My job
my boss
and me

My job my boss and me

Gaining control of your life

David Lee Woods

LIFETIME LEARNING PUBLICATIONS • Belmont, California
A division of Wadsworth, Inc.

Cover Designer: John Henry Hudson

Interior Designer: Michael A. Rogondino

Developmental Editing: Shirley Manning

Printed in the United States of America

1 2 3 4 5 6 7 8 9 10—84 83 82 81 80

Library of Congress Cataloging in Publication Data

Woods, David Lee.
  My job, my boss, and me.

  Bibliography: p.
  Includes index.
  1. Job stress.   2. Job satisfaction.
  3. Employee morale.   4. Success.   I. Title.
HF5548.85.W66   650.1   80–19829
ISBN 0–534–97982–3

This book is dedicated to all those who were there when I needed them, but most of all to the one person who has been central to my life. There is an Arabic saying, "A woman is not just a wife, she is your fate." I am thankful for Mary Jane, who has been my wonderful fate.

Contents

Why this book

I wrote this book because I wanted to share some of the insights I have gained from experiencing a difficult mental health problem that adversely affected my job performance. I have been extremely fortunate in regaining both my health and satisfaction in my work. I want to share my insights because I believe they can help others to recognize problems before they become too serious and because some of the processes I used to solve my problems may help others in solving similar problems.

This book is about some of the stresses involved in real management/subordinate relationships and describes both my own experiences and the experiences of others. There is no intention to imply that the actions of any specific individual led to any of the ideas or feelings expressed in the book.

I originally wrote about my own feelings to help me understand them better. At the urging of my friends, I have expanded this work in the hopes that it may help others to better understand both their own feelings and the feelings of those around them.

When it comes to feelings, the effects seem to be easier to see in others than in ourselves. Our self-image affects how we act, our actions influence how we are treated, and how we are treated affects our self-image; and so we are back at the beginning. I think that is why I have a great empathy for the crab. As a crab grows, it must shed its hard protective shell in order to get a new and larger shell in which to live. There have been times when I have felt bound in. But my rigid shell was made from the fibers of my own fears of trying something new in order to grow. I was afraid of being unprotected even for a little while.

I know at times I have clung with tenacity to the apparent safety of the status quo, unwilling to take even small opportunities to grow. But thanks to the help of others, I have been able to keep breaking my old rigid shells and keep growing as a person. For that help I extend my deepest thanks to those who have pushed and prodded me along the way. Without them I would still be a scared little boy inside a man with graying hair and a grandchild.

It has been said that the world can be divided into four groups of people—those who know what should happen, those who make it happen, those who watch things happen, and those who wonder what happened. I hope this book can help you know what should happen and then help you make it happen.

David Lee Woods
Livermore, California
June 1980

PART ONE

How stress feels when you're going down

Stress makes work much harder

I heard them say, "Cheer up, things could be worse," so I cheered up and sure enough things got worse. That bit of humor is really not very funny when it proves true and is in your own life. On the job we tell others to cheer up, that life can't be all that bad. But why are we really trying to cheer up the other person? In most cases we really just don't like to be with anyone who is down because it can bring back a lot of painful memories.

I think most of us find that it is easier to help another person if we can get a feeling for how far down he or she really is. We can also more easily help ourselves when we are down if we know just how far down we are.

There are many things that can get us down; however, this book is primarily about how stress on the job adversely affects us. This stress can be from the job itself, the boss, or from within ourselves.

Though we all live with some stress, too much adverse stress can be brought on by any of these three employment-related forces and can push us to the point where it is affecting our lives. These forces—our jobs, our bosses, and ourselves—are different but interrelated.

How our jobs can cause us stress

Our jobs may *not* be right for us and may *never* have been right, or we or our jobs may have changed. As an organization changes, many jobs change; as a job changes, a person's fit with the job may change.

Another real problem is that many of us just happened into our jobs. In school we took the courses we found interesting. However, just because a course is interesting does not necessarily mean that the person who has taken it will find working in that area to be interesting. We may have become bored with our area of specialty. A job without interest can drive most of us toward an undesirable level of stress. The right job is important for all of us who want to get more out of work than a paycheck.

But I have had jobs where I have lost interest not because of the subject but because of my own lack of personal growth. I let myself lose interest in the job, and as a result I did not show much enthusiasm for my work. Seeing this lack of enthusiasm, my boss was never sure how well I would perform a task, so I was not assigned as many challenging tasks. This, of course, cut my level of interest further and so I started on my downward spiral.

How our bosses can cause us stress

With any job comes a boss, and the boss can make a big difference in how much stress we feel. Over the years most of us have had many different bosses, and our feelings about each have been different. However, all bosses have one thing in common: like us, they are all people, people trying to do their jobs. And like us, they have human frailties and face each day's problems with some level of anxiety. Bosses have to worry about what their bosses want and how to meet organizational goals through the efforts of their subordinates. And for better or worse, boss and subordinate often add stress to each other's lives. Sometimes they feel good about each other, and then there are times things don't go as smoothly.

I can remember working for bosses who were themselves under a lot of pressure and who, because of the adverse stress in their lives, did not always make decisions and judgments that were in the best interest of the work group. I also know that at times my actions did not help relieve their stress. Sometimes my actions added stress to both the boss's life and to my own life.

How we can cause ourselves stress

Sometimes we create our own stress from within ourselves by letting ourselves overreact to pressures—pressures from work, from home, or from anywhere.

I know much of the adverse stress in my life has been of my own making. Nobody was doing anything *to* me, it was just a set of circumstances. When things did not go well, I went down instead of rising above the situation.

I now feel we can all learn to rise above any situation, no matter how bad it seems at the time. To be able to rise above adverse situations, we need to know not only ourselves but we also need to know how adverse stress can affect us. To learn about ourselves, we need to know when we are open to growth and when we are hiding from ourselves. Over the years I have been trying to feel more at peace with myself and I have also become more comfortable with others. I now understand a little more what is meant by the saying, "When you are at peace with yourself, any place can feel like home."

In addition to feeling at home at work, we all have a home and a life away from work. Home pressures are real and can compound a work problem, creating some tremendous stress in our lives. For the working mother or any working single parent, child care can create some real stress. Many women feel guilty about working and not staying home to care for their children. This guilt can be there whether they prefer to work or work of necessity. But it can tear out the heart of any parent to hear the sick child cry, "Please stay home today" when, in order to keep our job, we must go to work.

We don't really leave our kids at home or at the sitter's or at nursery school. They are always with us. I know I think about my children many times during the day. But I also know that we two parents together can work things out. For single parents, home pressure can add greatly to work pressures and will at times adversely affect work performance.

The stress of bereavement

Being alone after the death of a beloved spouse can affect us in many ways. We may have many self-doubts about our ability to cope with our children and the world now that we are all alone. After a death, each of us will grieve in our own way, and it is important that we be allowed to. When a co-worker has lost a spouse and then returns to work, it is hard to know what to say. Our reluctance to talk can add to their sense of loss. I have found that the easiest thing for me to do is ask, "How is it going?" and then give them time to answer in their own way. If they want to talk, I give them all the time they need. If they don't, I don't push. By not pushing I am respecting their ability to cope. All I am doing is assuring them that I care.

Bereaved persons who are older and have been married for many years have an additional problem. It is often very hard for such a person to accept that they are now, and always have been, a complete and separate human being. They now have to make a momentous choice between living a real life or just existing until death. With an understanding boss and co-workers, they can find the road back to life. To not show understanding and compassion would be an injustice.

The opposite of injustice is not justice, but love. And love can help us all. It has been said that the best medicine is love and if that doesn't work, double the dose.

When we are under a lot of stress, it is often hard to give or show love. It takes a very stable and understanding partner to withstand the effects of serious and prolonged stress at work. If the relationship is to survive, we must share our work problems with our partners so that we can cope and grow together.

I have read about men who were fired and just could not tell their wives. They would leave the house every day just as if nothing had happened, then spend the day looking for a new job. They faced their problem all alone with no one to talk to—except maybe a bartender. Their self-imposed exile did nothing except compound an already stressful situation. In most cases, the wife knew that the husband had lost his job but could not get him to talk about it. This, of course, added another round of stress to the marriage.

Just being open and honest with our partners can make a big difference in our lives. If we are open and honest about the little things, when the big things come up, it is easier to talk about them. Talking out problems can help keep our self-doubts from dragging us down to where we may feel of little worth to ourselves or to anyone else.

These self-doubts and feelings of being of little worth are themselves the most severe of all the pressures that affect us on or off the job. If we keep, or rebuild, our self-respect and our feeling of worth, we can come out a better person after any experience. We cannot change the experience, and the wounds to our mental health may take longer to heal than any physical injury needs. But we can make sure that we come out with a renewed and positive self-image.

Most of us know people who have come through some very tragic and traumatic experience to a new level of personal growth. We have also known people who gave up after a very minor incident.

Each of us can grow or die in the face of a bad experience. It is up to us. But the more we know about the adverse effects of stress, the better we are able to cope with future stressful experiences.

Understanding how stress can affect us

My job is designing industrial training courses, and my hobby is photography. Because I like photography, I find it very easy to spend excessive time in developing the visuals for a new course. However, developing the visuals is also a good place for me to hide when I feel a lot of pressure on the job. It is very easy for me to "justify" the excessive time I spend on them.

The important thing is for me to know how I feel about my hiding. If I still have perspective, and hide for just a little while, then I am still in control. After a break, I can restructure my priorities to relieve some of the pressures and then go back to work. On the other hand, if I can't see how to restructure my priorities, or I am unable to see what is bothering me, then I may be in trouble.

I can now look back at times when I would hide from tasks that were stressful for me. It wasn't that I didn't work hard—I think we all work the hardest when we are hiding. I now know that when I am doing something intensely, I need to stop and look at my reasons, but most important to look at my feelings.

I can remember being totally immersed in learning computer programming. I can also remember that I did not want to face a very stressful interpersonal problem that I needed to solve. By hiding in my computer programming I was able to avoid the problem. Of course, it simply got worse, and so my need to hide became even stronger. Things just started going from bad to worse because I would not face the stressful problem and try to solve it.

The pressure-paralysis reaction

One of the first signs that stress is adversely affecting us is the inability to set priorities. Then work pressure paralyzes our ability to make rational decisions. This pressure-paralysis makes us unable to distinguish the difference between the various pressures acting on us, and so we lump them all together as a single overriding force.

We may try to escape from the "single" pressure by escaping from them all. This escaping may show up not only in poor job performance but, in extreme cases, it can take the form of an ulcer or heart attack brought on by chronic tension; or excessive drinking, quitting a job with a hasty "shove it," explosive violence, or in some cases even suicide.

This type of reaction to stress is not necessary if we look straight at the cause of the stress, and then do something to make our lives less stressful.

To lower the pressure in your life, you need to be concerned and aware of the stresses that affect you—stresses caused by the things you do on the job, how you react with your boss, and most of all, how you feel about yourself. Any or all of these stresses can cause a pressure-paralysis type of reaction. Pressure-paralysis is not an off/on thing, but it does have a trigger point where it can start rapidly getting worse. You may be working near this level where you can easily go beyond the point of self-help. At this point, with just a small increase in stress, you may start the catastrophic buildup to extreme pressure-paralysis.

This pressure-paralysis can adversely affect our judgment as well as our actions. To help me find out what bothers me, I often make notes about how I am feeling or what someone may have said. Rereading these glimpses into my past gives me a new and broader perspective. As I look back I remember that old jingle, "Fly back, fly back, oh time in thy flight, I thought of a comeback I needed last night." I now know that I often needed more than a comeback. What I needed was a better understanding of how much the stress in my life was adversely affecting all of my behavior, both on and off the job. I have found my writing about myself to be one of the most effective things I have done to better understand me. My writing has become the key to unlocking a lot of secrets about me that I had been keeping from me.

You may also find it useful to write notes about and to yourself. It is easier to keep track of your notes if you use a notebook. But even if you just use scraps of paper, put the date on any note. The important thing is to write how you feel when you feel it. Just let the words flow and don't worry about how they will read later.

A friend gave me some of his notes to himself. Here is an example:

> There are just too many projects that "need" to be done but my boss gives me almost no guidance about setting priorities . . . then whenever I set a priority, the boss always says it was wrong. . . .

My friend felt rushed into doing tasks, yet he also felt he was wasting his time because he was always working on the wrong task.

Think about the pressures that are affecting you, the pressures from your job, your boss, and from within yourself. Then write some notes to yourself.

The effects of rushing through life

There have been times in my life when I have felt very rushed, times when my desk was cluttered with many different tasks that were all due NOW. Sometimes I felt good about being needed and the excitement of getting all the work done on time. There have been other times when I felt very depressed because I couldn't possibly get anything done on time. One day as I was rushing along I asked the question, "Why am I running and where am I going?" But alas, like many others, I did not like the question so I did not look for an answer, and just rushed off hither and yon. But I did take time to write:

The Pressure System

I feel guilty when I am not rushing,
pushing myself to near panic.

Yet there are moments when I can bask in the feeling
that there is nothing to do
that can't wait until later.

It feels great—
but somehow it doesn't feel right.

I don't know if I feel guilty
because I'm not pulling my share,
or whether I feel unworthy
of such a luxury.

I push myself,
but I don't know
what I am running from.

It is really hard to find work worthwhile when I am rushing around all of the time. It was this rushing that led to one of my first really "down" periods.

As we go through the part of our lives called employment, we experience both highs and lows. Some of these feelings come from our rushing to do things. Sometimes we rush for the sheer joy of the job, and sometimes it is because the job really needs to be done now. If you feel good about your job and you rush to do it, great; however, if you are rushing through tasks and this is adding adverse stress to your life, then this is not so good.

Feeling rushed can affect our sense of reality. I was once a passenger in a car when we were stopped at a crossing by a train. Even though there was plenty of time to keep our appointment, the driver was a nervous wreck after only two minutes when the train had cleared the crossing. He then drove at a terrifying speed as though we needed to make up the lost time.

I also remember late one night waiting in the hospital emergency room with one of my kids. A mother came in with a girl about nine years old who had a cut on her forehead. There was blood all over the child's face and clothes, but the bleeding had stopped. A nurse looked at the child and told the woman to wait. But the mother felt a strong need to rush; in fact, she was on the verge of panic. She kept saying "Hurry up! Hurry up! Why do I have to wait so long?" When they told her to come into the examination room, she asked in a loud, frightened voice, "What took so long?" She had lost touch with the reality of time. I had glanced at my watch and realized that the entire episode took just a little over three minutes.

When we feel rushed, minutes may seem like hours, the boss clearing his throat may sound like an admonishment, and a slammed door is a sign of anger.

Sometimes our need to rush may drive us into doing everything in a hurry. There are some tasks that do need to be done NOW. It would be bad news if firemen waited to finish their coffee before responding to an alarm. Responding to an alarm is one of the things that really does need to be done now. However, there are many tasks that truly do not need to be done in a rush. Accident/incident investigations have shown that when people hurry through activities, there is a far greater chance of making an error or overlooking something. I think this is even more so if we feel rushed and don't feel we can take time when it is needed. Even firemen must take time to do their jobs safely; an injured fireman cannot put out a fire.

Taking on too much

Why is it that there always seems to be enough time to do a task over, but seldom enough time to do it right in the first place? I think most bosses would prefer that jobs were done right the first time; but bosses are human and they keep asking for more and more in less and less time. They have pressures on them, pressures to get out more work. It is how we respond to our bosses' requests that is important. If we just keep taking on more and more work but do not say anything to the boss about our work load, the boss may never know how much we drive ourselves; and most bosses do not expect us to drive ourselves into adverse stress.

Even though the work does not need to be rushed, we sometimes just keep on rushing through it and our life. I have had subordinates who would take on any extra work and rush it through; however, I had to check everything for errors and there were often oversights. Other people who knew their limits would speak up when they were asked to do too much. Their work was always outstanding and there were few errors or oversights.

There is a difference between getting a lot of work done and the feeling of being rushed. Think back about how you felt when you did not have enough time to do a task as well as you would have liked to do it. Think about your feelings about your work and how these feelings may have adversely affected your ability to do your tasks to the best of your ability. Do you feel that you can speak up and say NO when you have too much work to do? Stress is like any problem; you can't start to solve it until you acknowledge that there is a problem. Take the time to think about the stress in your life and then write some notes to yourself about it. The act of writing about the problem will make it easier for you to control the feeling of stress.

I know a man who was starting to feel a lot of stress after he had been on a new job only a short time. He did the smart thing. He took a careful look at himself and his job situation. He then realized that he was the new person with a great deal more up-to-date knowledge than the rest of the work group had. Many of his co-workers had not kept pace with their fast-developing field. They felt the new employee was a threat to their job security and they took every opportunity to make him look bad. From this realization, he could start to work on his stress.

You *can* control the stress that is adversely affecting you when you know how you feel about what is affecting you, and then what to do about it.

Feeling pushed, stressed, and worse

For me it was neither the job nor the boss that was pushing me. In fact, my bosses and my co-workers said, "Slow down, what's the hurry?" But I did not hear them and rushed off, building up my own stress level.

I had a gnawing feeling that I should not be rushing, that I should slow down, so I took on a few extra things to do at home and called that relaxing. I still take on more jobs than I can possibly get done but I don't have that nagging feeling that I am being rushed. It is true that busy people get things done. They, however, are likely to feel a very exciting level of stress, not a debilitating stress.

When I wrote "The Pressure System" I felt that the need to rush was adversely affecting my work. Others seemed to be able to relax and do a good job. I felt that I had to rush to prove to someone (probably just to me) that I could do more work than anyone else. At this point, I had a choice—I could do something about the gnawing feeling that things were not right, or I could ignore the feeling. I chose to try to ignore it.

One result of feeling terribly rushed was to shortchange my family. There was one time when one of my daughters asked me whether she should have her old car fixed or buy a newer one. To fix the car would have cost at most $600 and would have given her dependable transportation. But I was too rushed to talk with her about the problem. The car she bought cost her over $6,000, including financing charges which she could ill afford. My feeling of being rushed cost her several thousand dollars. I also shortchanged one of my sons when he was in high school. He was playing junior varsity football and all of the games were in the afternoon. But I always felt too rushed over my work to take an afternoon off and see him play.

Now that I am away from the need for excessive rushing, I can see it in others. With two hours of commute time each day, I observe some drivers who seem to be rushing to their graves. They zigzag back and forth behind cars until there is almost enough room in the next lane, then with a quick lane change as brakes squeal they zoom off at high speed. For all the risks they take, they may save five or ten minutes on a fifty-mile commute. These speeding drivers come in two types, the ones who drive for sport and those who seem to feel rushed. The ones who drive for sport are just playing a big game with their own and other people's lives. They seem relaxed and enjoy the game. But the others, with white knuckles and grim expressions, must be exhausted when they get to work. If they run their day the way they drive, it is no wonder they feel stress.

A friend has told me of a period when he lived in a continuous state of apprehension and feeling of futility. He felt he would never catch up, but if he didn't hurry he would fall farther and farther behind. He had too many projects to do, and very little idea of their relative priorities. The net result was that he tried to second-guess his boss's priorities and often worked on the wrong project. Or, he tried to do them all and again he failed, increasing his feeling of personal inadequacy.

Like my friend and so many others, I have felt rushed
because I was being pushed both by my boss and by a
growing feeling of inadequacy, a feeling that told me I had to
prove my worth.

Now I can see that I should have listened when they
said, "Learn to pause or nothing worthwhile will ever catch
up with you." But I didn't and as I tried to ignore my feelings
that things were not right, I began to develop feelings of
uncertainty.

Uncertainties of life

I was uncertain why I was running; uncertain about my job
and my ability to do it, about my boss and how he felt about
me. This did not seem right, but I was even uncertain about
that.

Many of us have been uncertain about what our bosses
wanted. A friend talks about working for a super-bright,
super-achiever type of boss who was also super-critical. It was
almost impossible to do anything well enough to please this
boss. My friend also got the feeling that he dared not ask about
anything, for that would show an obvious lack of knowledge
and confirm the boss's opinion that he was incompetent.

I remember a time when there was a sudden increase in
the work load of my department and at the same time my
boss reduced the allowable turnaround time. When I
objected, the boss decided to cut my staff. We did not meet
the deadline and that fact loomed large when the time came
for my annual performance evaluation. By that time, I was
very uncertain about my ability to do my job.

As the level of uncertainty began to increase, I began to
think that a little uncertainty is good but a bunch is bad.
Then one day when I was feeling a bunch of uncertainty, I
wrote "Zest."

Of course some uncertainties are necessary because life is
a mystery to be lived, not a problem to be solved. But I think
at times we all are a little too uncertain about our jobs and
whether they are right for us, about whether the job has
changed or we have changed. We may all be a little uncertain

Zest

If uncertainty adds zest to life
    like chili peppers
    add spice to tacos

All is well
    'til the chili peppers
    get bigger than the tacos.

about our bosses and how they feel about us and about our work. When my daughter had nearly completed her probation period on a new job, she said she was getting a little worried. She thought she was doing well but her supervisor had never said how she was doing. Her supervisor was very surprised when she asked and then told my daughter that she not only was doing an excellent job but that she might soon get a promotion. My daughter had been concerned about an uncertainty in her life that was easily made certain, and so a little adverse stress was relieved.

I know I have let stresses about uncertainties build up when it was not necessary. I remember a time when the organization I was with was facing a reduction in force and I did not know whether I would be laid off. My boss had assumed that I knew that my job was solid, but he did not know that I felt a lot of adverse stress because I was uncertain about my job future. Because I did not ask, and he did not say, my stress level grew with each passing day.

Not really knowing how the boss feels can be stressful; however, if we want to relieve that stress situation, all we usually need to do is ask.

If you now feel as I did when I wrote "Zest," that there is too much uncertainty in your life, you have a choice. You can do something about it or you can ignore your feelings. I ignored my feelings. That was when I began to feel tired all the time, then exhausted. My work felt like a heavy load and I scarcely had the energy to move. I almost felt like a car stuck on a railroad crossing, while the approaching deadlines loomed like fast-moving freight trains.

Too many tasks

On top of my heavy load of work, I was exhausted from building an addition to our house. I can still look around the house at spots of shoddy workmanship and relive that feeling of "I don't care how it looks. I just have to go to bed." I remember coming home from work late on a cold night to a broken water pipe. And I also remember slumping down into the mud, sobbing, after I had cross-threaded a pipe fitting.

Raising children and the feeling of excessive job pressure also don't mix well. There were many times when I screamed at the kids over some little thing. These bursts of temper, of course, led to feeling guilty about being a bad parent and feeling frustrated at not being able to control myself.

Sometimes I am sure that it is better to give up and not finish a project than to try to reach impossible goals. There is a sand and gravel supplier in our neighborhood who had a cement mixer full of set concrete. The story goes that the man who rented it just reached a point of exhaustion where he said to hell with it and stopped working. In reality, the $200 he was charged for repairing the mixer may have been the best money he ever spent for his mental and physical health.

Stress can cause a lot of extra physical fatigue. I have a friend who felt such tension on the job that he suffered severe muscle tightness across the shoulders; the pain would last for hours after a rough session with his boss. He often got so exhausted that he just did not give a damn about the job.

Some work, by its very nature, may cause some individuals emotional injuries that take a long time to heal. I know a man who was a counselor at a chemical-dependency clinic. He realized that he himself needed to go through the program. Afterwards, he and his boss felt that he should take at least a year off in order to regain his perspective before he began counseling others again.

For me and many others, there is an extra problem at work in the spring of the year. April showers bring May flowers and the accompanying hayfever. A siege of hayfever will sap my strength, leaving little to withstand the onslaught of a negative work situation. But just being aware of the effects of hayfever adds a little certainty to my life.

Are your Monday morning blues getting a little bluer? Are you getting more uncertain about yourself, your abilities, your stability, your nerves? Maybe you are a little more jittery than you used to be, and the kids and the neighbor's dog get you down a little more. If this is how you are now, you can relieve some of the stress by finding ways to make your life a little more certain.

Little changes can help

To help make my life a little more certain, I began to make some changes both at work and at home. Some of my work habits, such as a messy desk, added to my stress-related uncertainties. I remember more than once when I knew I put "it" right there, but when "it" wasn't there and the boss wanted "it now," a lot of stress was added to my life.

My desk now seems to vacillate from very clean with everything in the files or wastebasket, to about four large piles that I go through in a panic. As my desk starts to pile up, I feel a little of that pressure-paralysis slowly gripping me. I also notice that the quality of my work starts to decrease as my desk mess starts to increase. Now I sometimes do as I did before—I let it go and ignore my feelings. But only for a little while, because I now know what those feelings mean. I do not let things get out of control: once to the bottom of the well was enough for me. I never again want to be the person I was when I was so totally exhausted that I could not figure out how to get the physical, mental, and emotional rest that I so desperately needed.

When I was at this point, everything seemed bleak and there didn't seem to be any excitement in my work activities. And because of my total exhaustion, my non-work life was beginning to deteriorate, so nothing in life seemed to be worthwhile.

When apathy sets in

One day at the beach with a friend we talked about the uncertainties in life. For her, the uncertainties had been almost too much. As we talked, a lot of my old feelings came back and I wrote "The Shore."

The Shore

I hear the surf
    and calling gulls
Like echoes of
    my anguished soul.

I see shore birds
    scurrying from surf.
As I run
    for all my worth.

I was running on and on, ignoring my feelings. Then something else happened in my life. All of the excitement gradually seemed to go away. There didn't seem to be anything worth looking forward to. As the popular song a few years ago said, "Is that all there is to life?"

I went on pretending that I was satisfied with my job, my boss, and with me. I reached a point where I could no longer tell what I liked and what I didn't like. One day I received a rather prestigious award for which I had worked very hard. I remember saying, "So what," and then I wrote "A Toast to Glory."

A Toast to Glory

When I was young and in my prime
    I used to dream most all the time
    of glorious accolades and
    ticker tape parades.

But now I'm older
    and my dreams decline,
I think that stuff
    is a waste of time.

I realized that I had been lying to myself about what I really liked to do. The feeling was beginning to grow that there was nothing exciting to look forward to, no new challenges, no new something that was worth the trouble. At this point I was working well enough but I was working only for a paycheck. It was the only thing that was important, I thought. But somehow I knew that I was being left out of a lot of things that could be exciting.

I remember in a "Life Planning" class trying to find where the excitement had gone. The class leader suggested that we try to remember some of the good things in life. I found it felt good to reminisce about weddings, births, and playing with the kids. I remembered good times that I had shared and good times when I was alone. There had been such times both at home and at work. Sometimes bad feelings had been mixed with good feelings. For example, I remembered a report I wrote and my boss said some negative things about it, and about me. However, I knew it was good and I felt good about it. I also felt good when, a few years later, he was using the information and commented that my report had been right. Until I started to remember the good times, I had almost forgotten what excitement felt like.

If the excitement in your life is going away and you wonder where it is going, you may find it helpful to remember as many good times as you can. The memories not only feel good but they help you to set goals for how you want your life to be again. Write yourself some notes about them.

Apathy and what you can do about it

For me, increasing apathy toward the job and decreasing self-image went hand in hand, and I know this is true for others.

A young man told me that he had been involved for several years with a cultic religious organization. Toward the end, he doubted the value of his work and himself, and became very apathetic. Before he joined the group he had been athletic and kept himself in fine shape. He said that as his apathy increased and his self-image decreased, he stopped exercising and started to eat more. He soon went from a trim 165 to a fat 285.

He later dropped from the group with many doubts about their teachings and even more doubts about his value as a human being. Now, a few years out of the group, he has even stronger negative feelings about certain cult activities and he also has very strong positive feelings about his own self-worth.

As my job performance deteriorated, the pressure to do a good job increased, pressure from both my boss and from within myself. As the pressure increased, my ability to make rational decisions decreased; and so things went from bad to worse.

I knew that I needed to find some way to break out of the apathy cycle but I could not seem to see what to do. I felt like the crew of a sailing boat that was becalmed during a race. Though I could see the well-fluffed sails of other boats, mine hung limp. I was feeling like this when I wrote "Becalmed on the Sea of Apathy."

Becalmed on the Sea of Apathy

Lifeless sails hang limp,
*   the rudder useless.*
The force of current and
*   wave direct a wayward course.*

It needs but a gentle breeze
*   to quicken the crew,*
Put new life in the rudder
*   to strain wheel and line.*

The sails need not be
*   taut before the gale*
Only fluffed
*   before a gentle breeze.*

And the crew will keep the craft
*   on course.*

The becalmed sailor may start his motor and go in search of a favorable breeze, or stay adrift and live with the way things are. The choice is yours. In my case, I found it was hard not to be apathetic about doing something about my apathy. However, I did start doing something. I tried just to add a little more excitement to my life, both at work and at home. When there was something to look forward to at the end of the day, either at home or at work tomorrow, it was easier to start working on my apathy toward life.

One focus of that "Life Planning" class I took was what

we liked to do with our spare time. Since I was beginning to doubt my professional ability, I decided to spend some of my time on the activities of one of the professional societies to which I belong. I volunteered for some committee work and later became an officer. I felt useful, and that was a tremendous counterbalance to the negative feelings I was experiencing at work. In retrospect, I think that this was a very important step in rebuilding my self-respect in my profession.

My concept of my worth as a person was also deteriorating. I needed to hear people say, or at least imply, that they liked me. To bolster my feeling of worth as a person, I became involved in youth group activities. Youngsters are very honest in their feelings about us. When they show warmth it can be very reassuring to an adult. The many weekends and weeks of vacation time I spent as a youth leader were very good for me. The kids and other adult leaders helped me to keep up my feeling about my worth as a person.

Another source of help was the beauty and balance of nature. In nature I searched for serenity and I did the hunting with my camera. This had a different effect on me than my other activities. In my professional society, my colleagues told me, "You can do a good job." In my service activities, the children told me, "We like you as a person." My family told me, "We love and need you." But in my search for aesthetic understanding, I said to myself, "I like what I find and I like how I feel, and because of this I am growing as a person."

To help get rid of my apathy I also tried to share my feelings. This started just by talking about my likes and dislikes, at home and at work. I was surprised by comments such as, "I didn't know you liked to do that." Comments like this came from my boss, co-workers, spouse, and even my kids.

It helps to talk about your feelings

If you have never talked to someone about how you really feel, it is scary when you first get started. The other person has to be someone you can trust and trust completely. This

may be a close friend or, if you don't have a friend who is
really close, it could be a professional counselor. Many
companies now have counseling services for employees. Many
social and religious organizations also have counselors
available to both members and non-members. Even the
phone book can be a source of help with its lists of counseling
services under such headings as Marriage and Family
Counseling, Personal Service Bureaus, Psychologists, Social
Services and Welfare Organizations, Social Workers, and
Suicide Prevention. However, it's a much better idea to have
a counselor that someone you know recommends. If your
organization has employee assistance counselors, you need to
make an appointment *and keep it*.

In many cases people who are very apathetic about work
are much like people with a drinking problem. Until they
admit that they have a problem, no one in the world can help
them.

There are different types of help we can get from
counselors and there are different kinds of counselors. One
kind can help us get a grip on our own psychological stability.
It is much better to go to a counselor on our own than it is to
have them come and get us. At this stage all the jokes about
the men in white coats are no longer funny, and they may
even be frighteningly real. I have two friends who were
committed for psychiatric counseling; one came back, the
other did not.

The other type of counseling is career counseling. It can
help us determine if we are really in the right job, where
we can get help to change jobs, and how to know what kind
of a job we should be seeking. The unfortunate thing is
that we often feel very trapped because of both economic
needs and the ego need to say, "Not me—I could not have
failed."

If I were down there again I would try to make a list of
all of the various sources of help. Even if I didn't need them,
it would be comforting to know where to go for help if I did
feel I needed it. I would look up the Suicide Prevention
phone number and carry it with me. We never know how
close we are to needing this service in a hurry. I never
needed it but eventually I did accept the fact that I needed
some counseling, both psychologically and in terms of job

placement. I received this counseling help through my company's employee assistance program.

I guess I was reluctant to get involved with psychological counseling because I had always been under the impression that it took months or even years to be of any value, and even then the results may be dubious. But in this case, I needed only three one-hour sessions about two weeks apart and then one follow-up session about two months later.

Who really has the problem?

Talking to a neutral, non-threatening person who is skilled at counseling was a very important step for me. However, I had a dear friend who apparently has never admitted that he has a problem. Whenever we talked it was always "them out there" who were doing things to him. He has spent the last fifteen years in and out of psychiatric wards and psychiatrist's offices. I haven't seen him for several years but from what I've heard, there doesn't seem to have been any improvement—"they" are still to blame.

Sometimes it is very hard to admit that we are the ones with the problem. It is much easier to blame it on someone else. I know a couple who were separated after seven years of marriage. She was very levelheaded and mature when they married; he was 24 going on 14. When they separated she had been able to get and hold responsible jobs while he, even with advanced degrees, was doing menial part-time work. But worse yet, he was now 31 going on 17. He told me one day after the separation that his wife needed to do a lot of growing up and he probably needed to grow a little. He has never accepted the fact that he is the one with the problem. Until he can, he will never be able to overcome his immaturity and fit into a workable marriage.

One difficulty in admitting that we may have an emotional or mental health problem is that we feel such a problem is not generally socially acceptable. But about one-fourth of all beds in U.S. hospitals are occupied by mental patients, and about one in seven people who visit doctors with *physical* complaints have *emotional* problems that are partly or wholly responsible.* Still, most of us feel that this is all happening to the other guy. It is difficult to accept the fact that the other guy may be us. Why? There are so many jokes and social taboos against people who are "crazy" that we do not want to be one of them.

In fact, there is no one who is "normal"; we are all a little crazy in some ways. A counselor can help reassure us that we are hardly crazy at all. We may have anxieties that have no apparent cause. There are times when my boss has been so busy he didn't even say "Good morning." At other times he has been very upset with something that had nothing to do with me. Yet I feel some anxiety at these times about my relationship with my boss. I also have fears about other things. I will not ride on a motorcycle or a skateboard, and I know people who will never go up in an airplane. Some people turn pale and break out in a cold sweat at the prospect of receiving *any* radiation. They refuse to have even a dental X-ray. They turn deaf ears on any discussion about the level of risk.

Are these fears exaggerated? Not to the persons who have them. It is not the fear but how it affects us that is important. If the need were great enough, I would take a ride on a motorcycle even though I am sure that my nervousness would keep me from enjoying the ride.

Fear can fence us off from the rest of the "offending" world. The fence may be made of daydreams or TV. We may become super-competitive to prove our worth, or attack "them" as being unworthy.

One fear about psychological counseling rests on a question in many employment application forms: "Have you ever had psychotherapy?" Of course, we all *know* that if you answer "yes," you will *never* get the job. Is this an unreasonable fear? I hope so but I am not sure. Unfortunately, many people are also not sure, so they do not seek professional help when they really need it. *Not* getting the help may do far more to keep us from getting a job than getting help and answering "yes" to that dreaded question.

---

*What Everyone Should Know About Mental Health, Greenfield, MA: Channing L. Bete Company, 1980.

If you are down there—you must act

Damn it! Do something about it before it's too late. Make
some changes, get help, talk to a counselor, make life worth
living. Don't do as I did and ignore your feelings. I made it
back from near the bottom—many do not. You may not
because it is hard to make changes in your life when you are
feeling trapped. The farther down you go, the harder it is to
change and the longer it will take for the hurt to heal. You
may lose your job, your family, your health, or even your life.
CHANGE NOW. With help you too can make it back to the
good life, a life when each day is worth living.

You don't have to be somebody else

After I had been ignoring my feelings for awhile, I began to
feel that I was not worth anything. My judgment, my skills,
my abilities were all of little value. I was less than adequate
as a person. At this point I started pretending to be what I
was not, trying to please others and not myself. How the boss
felt about me was most important; of course, I could only
guess how he felt. But since I knew it was bad, any little
signs of disapproval I remembered and amplified, and any
words of praise I did not believe. So I desperately sought
recognition of my worth as a person but when it came, I did
not believe it.

   I tried so hard to be what I ought to be that I forgot who
I was. One time when I was feeling as if I were playing a role
that I didn't understand, I wrote "A Mask Transparent."

   At times we all wear masks and play roles. We do or say
or wear what we think others expect us to. There is no
question that certain conventions govern all of our behavior,
but when we blindly follow them we may be in trouble.
Many jobs require a uniform that makes it easy for the public
to identify the workers and the functions they perform. But
many of us succumb to the uniforms we think will make us

A Mask Transparent

A mask can diffuse,
but it cannot hide
The soul that lies
so deep inside.

I cover myself
and try to hide,
But who I am is clear
to all outside.

Yet I pretend to be
what I am not
And wear a mask—
to protect what I've got.

look the part. An example is the person newly promoted to
supervisor who now wears a dress and heels or white shirt
and tie. Even the phrases "blue-collar worker" and "white-
collar worker" imply a type of uniform. The thing to be
concerned about is how much we let our feelings about
our dress influence how we dress.

I can remember when I felt very uncomfortable going
anywhere without a tie. I needed to have people see me and
think, "He's a member of management." Of course, I didn't
know what they really thought but I assumed they said, "He's
okay." I now find it interesting to go to a resort area and see
people wearing dress clothes where sport clothes or even blue
jeans would be more than adequate. When I look at them I
see a little of me wearing the label that tells everyone I am
what I am not. Now that doesn't mean there's anything wrong
with dress clothes or a uniform. But off-duty, if we still need
to wear our uniforms to impress on other people that we have
arrived, then in our own minds we may not have arrived. If
we find ourselves wearing a label that says, "Look, I have
arrived, I am somebody," we should try to look at ourselves
and see if we are wearing a mask. It has been said that "If
you need a label, you ain't."

I think it is important for all of us to ask ourselves whether we feel as if we are acting a part. Do you feel you don't belong? If you do, you may want to find out why, find out what has happened to cause you to feel this way.

The mirror does not have to lie

I think we wear masks when we do not like what we see in the mirror and we may feel that nobody else would ever like us if they knew the real us. So what do we do if we wear a mask? We have a choice: we can find out about our masks and learn to take them off a little at a time, *or*, since we don't like the mask we wear, we can try a new mask. Of course, the new mask won't work any better than the old one but at least it keeps us trying. To take off your mask you must try to see yourself as others tell you that they see you. It is important to consider the difference between what you see or think you see and what others say they see.

How do you separate your mask from the real you? How do you find out who you really are? You can start slowly by talking with a trusted friend or a counselor about what you are really like. Talk about some of the things that you were proud of. Don't talk about all of the bad things that went wrong but rather about the things—often little things—that you feel good about.

Only by sharing the inner parts of us a little at a time can we get to know ourselves a little better and to grow up as a person.

Of course, if you don't want to share any of you and don't want to shed your mask, you can do as I did and just keep on fighting the world—and fighting all alone. I wrote "The Lone Warrior" as I watched a friend go through a very stressful period. As I saw him I could re-live how I felt as I stood and fought all alone.

I remember the helplessness expressed on the faces of my friends as I fought that lonely, lonely battle. I felt all alone among my co-workers, even while we laughed and talked.

The Lone Warrior

The warrior
no longer knows
friend from foe.

Bruised and battered—
his back to the wall
his shield held close
his vision blurred
by blood, sweat, and tears.

Slashing out
at all who come near—
his friends dare not help
for fear that they too
will be struck down.

Helplessly they watch
as he faces his foes
all alone.

Your self-image must be reborn

When I was down, I think I must have come across like a wet blanket. I can remember going into a room where my co-workers were in a light-hearted mood. Yet when I had been there for a short time, the mood became somber and the group depressed. It wasn't that they didn't like me. They were just trying to ignore me, as I've often ignored people who were glum.

When we have been down and have lost interest in our jobs and maybe even our total lives, we must find a way to start building a new self-image. We, in reality, need to become a new person. We can do this by letting a little of our real self emerge so that it can grow. This of course can be a little scary because we often don't know what the new "me" is going to be like. I know now that I like the new me better than the old me. But most of all, once I started to let me out and let me grow as a person, life has become very exciting.

Conceiving a "new" you in your mind is actually a matter of being willing to let the real you grow. This growth period may be short or long, depending on how aware you are of your inner feelings. You will feel reborn when you have regained your positive self-image and are ready to face the world. This rebirth is based on who you are and what you like to do. From this comes a new concept of what you want to be. Then you will learn to believe that the new you is really you. And then you are ready to be reborn into a new job in a new organization, or be born again in the eyes of your current boss. To succeed at work you must become a new person in your boss's eyes, with new ability and new promise. That will bring back lots of excitement to your job.

What happens if you do nothing?

Of course we can all say we don't want to talk about our feelings. We can try to ignore them or keep lying to ourselves that it really doesn't matter how we feel about our jobs, our bosses, or our self-image. But it does, because we are on the way down—and down is not a good direction to go.

With twenty years in a retirement system and some obsolete skills, we may feel cozy but in a trap. We can't go out because we will lose all that retirement pay and we know we can never find a job "out there." We know we are not very good any more, so we do not want to face the disappointment of being turned down if we start looking. And we don't dare tell our bosses because we know they will not understand.

On the way down we may start to feel that we can't get out and can't stay in. Though I felt trapped when I wrote "A Toast to the Future," I did not get out—but I should have.

My boss had suggested that I attend a career planning program. At the time I did not believe the boss was really trying to help, but now I think he really was. Except he had a problem: it is hard to help someone who doesn't know how to help himself. I attended the career planning sessions, though I did not gain as much as I could have because I was so throughly trapped and lost in my own maze.

A Toast to the Future

Career planning is the way to go
for the future I would
surely know.

To bask in glory would be
just great,
But a staff job has become
my fate.

I've been told:
If you can't do it right,
don't do it at all.

But if I don't do it at ALL,
I fear the ax
will surely fall.

I'm sure my plight is not unique;
to survive to retirement
is all I seek.

When I wrote this I really thought I could make it all the way to retirement. But since I had no interest in life then, would anything have changed when I retired? The sad truth is that many people die within a few years after they retire. Is that what you want?

If you are on the way down, you need to take that first positive step to stop your downward slide toward desperation. It may be just one counseling session or making some small change in your home life. If you ignore your feelings and take no action, as I did, you may stop caring about other people, your job, your home, or even your life.

Some people seem to disappear within themselves, just staring at the TV, a birdcage, or a bottle and becoming more and more oblivious to the outside world. On the job they may do their work as if in a hypnotic trance, and in fact they can often do repetitive tasks quite well. However, if there is a change or an emergency situation, they may not be aware; they may make oversights that could damange equipment or injure themselves, or someone else.

The trip down to depression is not a smooth ride. Times of not caring are interrupted by moments of deep caring coupled with intense feelings of guilt for not having cared enough.

I don't remember when I reached the point where I stopped looking beyond the task of the moment and that never-ending pile of paper. I do remember when I no longer interpreted policy and procedures but simply followed them blindly. If the procedure said a task was to be done in a certain way, then that was the way it was done, regardless of any reason to make an exception. By-the-book decisions are often necessary; however, they are not really decisions at all—not when evaluation and interpretation are needed.

I remember a friend who sent his application to a college and had it returned with a letter explaining that the college now had a policy that all applications must be sent by registered mail to assure the delivery. Of course, by the time he got the letter and sent it back, he had to pay a late fee.

Have you ever followed the book, even if it did not make any sense, but you did not care any more? I remember beginning to feel that making decisions by the book was more important than getting the job done. That feeling is expressed in "The Paper Mover."

The Paper Mover

The paper comes in piles
and goes in dribbles.

I do my thing and pass it on;
if in doubt—
I go by the book.

If there is anger—
I do not look.

I do not mean, of course, that all by-the-book decisions should be avoided because someone gets upset. But when we lose the smile in our voices, the understanding in our explanations, our feelings of compassion for the person affected by our decision, then we are in trouble. We are not necessarily in trouble with the person affected, or the boss, but we are in trouble with ourselves. We have started to deny the existence of a part of ourselves—a very important part—our feelings. That's the part that makes life worth living.

At this point you must start talking to someone but don't get yourself into the trap of talking to others who may feel the same as you do about the job. If you do, you may all just keep saying "ain't it awful" and all keep on going down together. If you are looking in the telephone book for a counselor to talk to, you will find many more listings under "cocktail lounges" than under "counselors." There are many experts out there who can help you hide from yourself or help you find yourself. The choice is yours.

Talking with the boss

We may feel we have an S.O.B. for a boss, but our bosses may also feel that they have some S.O.B.s for subordinates. All relationships are a two-way street—it takes two to make love or to fight.

Later in this book is a description of how this subordinate felt as he lived through a degenerating boss/subordinate relationship. There is no attempt to point the finger at who is at fault. But of course, from the point of view of the employee who's in a tailspin, it is always the boss.

If you are not too far down into depression, you may be able simply to tell your boss that you would like to make some minor changes in your job assignment, that you feel you would do a better job as a result. Your boss is not a mind reader and he or she may not know that you have lost that certain spark unless you start to do the talking.

And if the boss asks, "How are things going?" tell him or her. The question may be asked because the boss senses that you are unhappy and really wants to help. Look at it from the boss's point of view. Have you ever tried to tell someone that they needed mouthwash? If you think that is rough, try telling someone that you think they should see a counselor because they seem to have lost that certain spark for life. You may not be able to make any changes now, but just knowing someone cares can make a big difference.

I have seen some very good people leave an organization when it may not have been necessary. Both they and their bosses had stopped trusting, then stopped listening, then stopped talking, and finally stopped caring. At this point someone had to leave, and it wasn't the boss.

How our bosses act and react

If you are apathetic about most of your work but are earnestly looking for some of that old spark, how do your actions appear to your boss? If you feel apathetic about your job, your boss, or about yourself, you might want to write some notes for yourself on how you feel. I find writing is crystallized thinking. Making notes about my feelings gives me a clearer understanding of them. When I can see me a little clearer, I can see better where I want to go. And if I don't decide where I want to go, I may end up some place else.

You may also want to think about how you look to your boss and how your boss treats you. While I had lost my enthusiasm for my job, at the same time I was desperately looking for some excitement in my work. Of course this type of behavior resulted in a very uneven level of job performance, and from my boss's point of view, I was very unpredictable. As my behavior changed, so did the way my boss treated me.

Actions always speak louder than words. How we feel about our job, no matter what we say, will show very clearly because our actions will tell our bosses how much we really enjoy our work. Our bosses may listen to what we say but they must interpret what our actions mean, and then decide how to help us become more effective subordinates. How our bosses look at us and treat us will depend on our boss/subordinate relationship. This relationship in turn depends on a number of different factors but mostly on how each of us feels both about ourself and about the other.

When the boss changes

The boss may change the way he or she behaves for reasons that have nothing to do with us, but the change can affect our relationship. After all, the boss is a subordinate to the next level up and may be experiencing a change in that subordinate/boss relationship. Our job description may change and the need to interact with our boss may increase or decrease. Or we may be the one who has changed and is causing a change in our relationship with the boss.

There is also the case where we may be doing just fine on our job, and then the boss leaves and we get a new one. This change can be traumatic for us if the new boss is very different from the previous one.

I know an elderly man who worked as a caretaker at a youth camp. He had been there forever and was as much a part of the camp as the trees and cabins. His pay was low, but he lived at the camp and loved it and the kids and the leaders. Everybody loved him. Then two things happened at once. His wife died and he got a new boss. He was very old and could no longer do hard work, but there were always many strong young people to do that work for him. But the new boss wanted a caretaker who didn't need to walk with a cane and could do the work. The new boss thus changed the job description and told the old caretaker he would have to leave. The double shock of losing his wife's love and then the love of all the hundreds of kids was just too much for him. He had liked a little wine with dinner but now he started having a little wine with breakfast. Though he stayed on at the camp through the influence of his many friends, he began to fear that he would soon lose his home. He found it more and more difficult to put down the bottle. Some day, of course, he will have to go, but when he does he will be warmed by the love of the kids and youth leaders who are better people just because they have known him.

There are many managers who look at a job as being more important than the person who does it. But people do have to matter even for these managers. Each job is more than the end-product; it is also a process that can be accomplished only by a person. And all individuals have feelings that affect how they do their work.

Our feelings and our interests change as we get older. Even though I don't like the idea of getting older, I think it is a lot better than the alternative. But as our interests change, we can become apathetic about our work. That will almost certainly change the way we interact with our boss.

The boss's job

Bosses have to get specific tasks done effectively and efficiently by using the skills and talents of their subordinates. That's us. We respond by doing our jobs in ways that could be rated: much better than needed, very good, adequate, less than adequate, wrong, or not at all. I think all of us sometimes do some parts of our work in each of these ways.

The boss may ask us to do something that is very exciting to us, so we give it our all and do a bang-up job. This is our chance to show the boss how good we really are. But what happens? We may do the task far more thoroughly than is needed, spending so much time on it that we only have enough time to do a so-so job on other tasks, or not even do them at all. What did we show our boss? That depends on the boss but some may say we did not do anything right. On our fun task we did far more than was needed, and on the other tasks we did less than was needed. We thought we were going great but the boss may evaluate our overall performance as less than adequate. Why did everything seem so right and turn out wrong?

Like children, adults find it very easy to blame someone else for all their problems. If your household is like ours, you have some strange kid named "He-Did-It" who lives there, and he has two friends named "Nobody" and "I-Don't-Know." These are the same mythical people adults can blame for all of their misfortunes. However, no matter how much we try to deny it, we are still responsible for our own behavior; and our behavior does influence the way other people feel and think about us, and of course how they act toward us.

What might happen if you walk in and say, "Boss, I seem to be losing some of the enthusiasm I had for my work"? That would depend on the type of boss you have. I use the words "might happen" and not "will happen" because I have no idea what your boss would really do. I don't even know what my boss would do, but since I would be demonstrating that I wanted to be enthusiastic about my work, I think he would want to talk *with* me. In fact, my boss started to do something *to* me the other day and I told him that I thought we had previously decided to do that activity together. He agreed, and we started over and did it together. If I had not spoken up I would have been "done unto" and my feelings would have been hurt.

A boss may generally feel very positive about us or may have some negative feelings. But there are four basic ways that our bosses may act toward us. They may do things TO us, FOR us, WITH us, or WITHOUT us. Even though the specific activity we are doing may determine how our boss acts toward us, the main determinant is how we feel about ourselves and about each other. The following is an oversimplified view of how our bosses may treat us. In real life, probably few bosses really think in the narrow way that I portray, and few of us subordinates usually act in the narrow way I describe.

Bosses who do things TO us

The boss who does things TO us also gets messages from us. When we are apathetic toward our work, we display indifference to it. Like warm robots, our faces are without expressions. During discussions we show no emotions, saying only yes or no or responding in the words from a computer: "Message received, does not compute, check data and repeat, that is all." If we act like a machine, our bosses may do things TO us in the same way they do things to a machine. We will encourage our bosses to be McGregor Type "X" managers or Blake 1,9 managers.* This type of manager seems to believe that people do not like to work, will only do what they have to, and then only when enough pressure is applied to get them to do their work.

When bosses are doing things to us, it is as much an attitude as it is actual acts. They tell us what to do and when to do it; we are not asked what we think.

It doesn't matter who starts the problem. We need to do our best to be treated as persons and not machines.

One of my sons worked in the shipping/receiving department of a large hardware store. He came home one day very upset. The new store manager had told him how he was to change the way he handled the incoming and outgoing material.

The manager had never worked in shipping/receiving and only knew what was done in other stores. There was no discussion; the boss just said, "Do it my way." He treated the people as if they had no ability to think. What he didn't know was that what he had "ordered" and not "suggested" had been tried before and, because of the way the building was laid out, it just would not work. All of the employees knew that. They tried to act like people but they were treated like machines, so they soon started to act like machines.

Often the boss does things TO people at pay raise time. The merit raise may be less than expected—and the explanation less than satisfactory. When this happens, most people harbor hurt feelings and take a long time to get over them. There are several possible explanations of a pay freeze apart from a boss deciding that the subordinate's work is below par. A person's job may be "red circled" and no raise

---

*McGregor, D. The Human Side of Enterprise. New York: McGraw-Hill, 1960; and Blake, R. B. and Mouton, J. S. The Managerial Grid. Houston: Gulf Publishing, 1964.

allowed for several years. Or a layoff may force a transfer to a lower paying classification where the individual's salary is frozen for awhile, if not cut. If the employee is not a party to the discussion and the boss just says, "Take it or leave it," that boss does things TO people.

I know someone who was teaching in an elementary school and the principal decided that some of the teachers were in a rut. His solution was to randomly switch the teachers' grade levels, with no discussion and no consideration of what the teachers wanted. The principal also decided to move one of the teachers to a different classroom. She found out about it when another teacher came over to help her with the move.

Making a list of the TO's

Writing notes to yourself about the things your boss does TO you can give you a better perspective. Sometimes when you read them over later, you can honestly say that an action was trivial and you can cross it out of your notes. On the other hand, some of the actions may leave you with a sense of grievance. Then you may feel you just have to talk with the boss, and the notes you have made will make that a lot easier.

There have been times when I was upset and tried talking with my boss. However, he was very skillful at changing the subject and when the meeting was over, I realized that we had not discussed some of the things I was upset about. At the next meeting he would say that the other problems must not have been very important because I never mentioned them in our previous meetings. When I used a list I was able to make sure we covered everything I wanted to talk about. At other times when I have wanted to talk with my boss, he was just too busy. Later he would drop by my office and have time to talk; but by then I would be deeply engrossed in a project and as we talked I would forget what I wanted to talk about. Having a list has proven to be helpful.

For best results, include everything you want to discuss and all of the supporting data, not just your gripes. There is also a fringe benefit of working from notes. You appear both well organized and serious about what you wish to discuss.

Whether or not you make a list, you may want to talk to your boss about your job. "The squeaky wheel gets the oil." So the boss that does things TO you, that is, thinks of you as a machine, will at least want to fix the machine that squeaks. I would approach this type of boss with the suggestion that I could be more efficient if I could make certain specific changes. I would outline the changes and precisely what I wanted my boss to do.

Bosses who do things FOR us

Bosses that do things FOR their subordinates will respond differently to the subordinate who is apathetic; however, the results may feel about the same to everyone in the work group.

People sometimes tend to do things for those who can't do for themselves. The little old lady helped across the street may have gotten help whether she needed it or not. Bosses who do things FOR people take the paternalistic approach to management; it is "we" and "they." The bosses, they know what is best, and we don't know what is good for us.

It has been said that there are the good and the bad, and the good decide which is which; we should also remember that Golden Rule which states, "Whosoever controls the gold writes the rules." If we show apathy toward our work, that only goes to prove we are incompetent to make decisions about it. So the paternalistic boss will make decisions FOR us. This boss will decide what we like, what we will do, and when.

To the paternalistic boss, we are at least more than warm robots; we are now incompetent children who need to be told what to do. As one child said to another, "A sweater is something you put on when your Mom is cold."

In some cases the boss may treat everyone like a child, and in other cases only a few may be treated as if they don't know what is good for them. However, how we are treated is to a large extent based on how we act as if we want to be treated. If we seem incompetent, we may find our bosses making some major decisions about our jobs and our future.

As an industrial training specialist, I have been involved in decisions about how individuals should improve their job performance. The paternalistic boss will tend to say, "Send so-'n-so to that course because it will be good for him/her." There is seldom any concern about what the person is interested in doing: it is generally, "He/she needs it."

Job assignments are sometimes handled in the same way. I have a friend who remarked to her department head that she was getting bored with her job. On the spot her boss transferred her to a different job so that she wouldn't be bored. There was no discussion about what she really wanted or whether her new supervisor wanted her for the job opening.

If you feel that your boss is doing things FOR you, again you may find it helpful to make notes about some specific examples, and how you feel.

You may also want to talk to your boss about your work. I would open the conversation with this "Father knows best" type of manager by asking for help—specific things that I need and suggestions on ways my job could be made more exciting so that I could do it better.

Bosses who do things WITH us

The boss who does things WITH us will be very unhappy with our apathetic performance. That boss looks at us as adult equals. In her or his eyes, the job of managing is different but not necessarily superior to our jobs. We diminish both us and the boss who sees us as equals when we do not perform our jobs as well as we can. This boss is genuinely disappointed when we are not up to our best. Of course, there is a limit to how much time and energy our bosses can spend on feeling disappointed with our performance. The work we do may still be adequate, but if we are less than enthusiastic our bosses may find very few things of interest to talk with us about.

I can remember periods when my boss seemed to have no more time for me. We had started some projects together and then I began to feel he had abandoned me. There is a difference between feeling set free and abandoned. As we go down, our bosses seem to go away from us, leaving us more and more alone.

When a boss does things WITH us, it implies that we are respected for our intelligence, judgment and interest, and that we have a right to have a voice in our destiny. On a good team everyone is respected, has a place, a job, and knows that what they are doing is worth doing. Team management by doing things with people does not imply that any of us should always get our own way, for obviously we all have different opinions. Someone has to make the final decision on how something will be done. However, each of us can feel that we are all part of the decision and that we all had a voice in it.

Working WITH a boss is a lot more fun than being done unto. I have found it helpful in this situation to be very clear about what each person expects the other to do, and when. One very important support that such a boss and the staff member can give each other is to share the work according to individual strengths and weaknesses. Since we are not all excellent at everything, nor do we like to do everything, this team sharing can help get the best work done fast. It starts with agreement on priorities and deadlines for tasks, and agreement on where help with the work can be obtained if it is needed.

I would approach this type of a boss with specific suggestions on how to make the team more efficient. These changes would, of course, include what I felt I needed so I could be more efficient and get more excitement out of my work.

Bosses who do things WITHOUT us

If we don't talk to the boss, we may feel more and more alone and become more like a machine. Then the boss may start doing things WITHOUT us—such as deciding with other managers whether our assets as employees are worth our liabilities.

Our boss may spend less and less time talking with us, or there may never have been anything interesting in common to talk about. Our boss may also do things WITHOUT us because he or she does not understand us.

It has been said that the worst sin toward our fellow creatures is not to hate them, but to be indifferent to them. When bosses do things WITHOUT us, they tend to ignore us. We just do our job and no one seems to care. The boss may decide to reorganize the work that the department does and, since we don't seem to exist, we may be among the first without work.

When you feel your boss doesn't seem to know you exist, you need to do something to improve the situation. You need to know whether your boss just has different interests or is deliberately ignoring you. If it is deliberate, you may also find the boss tending to make fun of you or to make you the scapegoat. There comes a point when even your slightest error or misjudgment is amplified and laughed about.

Of course, bosses may be so busy with their own problems that they don't take the time to go over things with us. When this happens, they may have the highest respect for our work but not feel that it is necessary to talk to us about it.

Whatever the cause of a boss doing things WITHOUT us, it is very important that we know whether it is a good sign or a bad sign. Our bosses, like all of us, are more comfortable with some people than with others. An action-oriented boss is more comfortable with people who get things done and not as comfortable with those who like to chat. If you like conversation, this boss may be a little short with you. On the other hand, if the boss is people-oriented, conversation will be more likely; if you happen to be action-oriented, you may seem offensively abrupt to this boss. Some bosses concern themselves with general concepts while others like to worry about the nitty-gritty details. If your way of thinking about things is different from the boss's, then you will be treated differently than someone who thinks as the boss does.

There is one type of boss, however, that we should all be wary of. That is the person who looks like Dr. Jekyll to those higher in the hierarchy and like Mr. Hyde to those lower down.

Talk with others—with care

After you have observed how your boss thinks, then observe how she or he treats other people. Talk to your friends in the organization, co-workers and the department secretary, to get their ideas about the boss. In every organization there is a grapevine that passes information far faster than any official system. One person I know claims that he could start a rumor and it would go to all three of his company's plants and be back in less than an hour. Somehow I never felt I could trust him enough to tell him of any problems I was having with my job. But he might certainly be able to give me useful information about my boss.

So ask around, but use discretion.

Whether you have a boss that does things TO you, FOR you, WITH you, or WITHOUT you, it is important to talk to your boss. The odds are high that such a talk will increase your understanding of each other. If, however, you don't make much progress, it may be that the boss is simply uncomfortable with such talks. Or the boss may purposefully not tell you how he or she really feels about you and your work. This would be a possibility if there were a plan to transfer or de-hire you.

Knowing when the end is near

I could not believe that my world, my make-believe world, the world where I thought I wanted to be but did not seem to fit, was all coming down around me. Every task I did seemed to turn out to be less than adequate. I had reached a point where I no longer ever felt the triumph of success, even a little success over little things. I could see the anguish in the eyes of my friends. I now know that I was being de-hired.

The de-hiring process

De-hiring is a process where the bosses can't fire you so they make your working life a living hell in the hopes that you will quit. De-hiring is used when an employee is doing an adequate enough job that a case can't be built to fire him or her for cause. Although de-hiring is often a very conscious and planned activity on the part of the bosses, it may be something they do very skillfully without even thinking about it. It may even be something that just happens. We need to remember that the boss has a vested interest in the employee because, if the work is not getting done or could be done better, the boss stands accountable. The boss must either get the subordinate to improve performance, or get rid of the subordinate.

Sometimes employees simply no longer fit into the changing organization because their technical skills have deteriorated or become obsolete. Their inability to fit in could also be caused by a change in bosses. A new boss may have a completely different set of interests, beliefs, and values than they have. A situation can deteriorate rapidly when a supervisor and a subordinate do not see eye to eye, and the supervisor is always right. Subordinates may also lose their effectiveness because of deteriorating physical or mental health.

Any of the above or other situations can lead to an organization starting the de-hiring process, either by design or by default. I had a neighbor who was working for his father-in-law. Everything was fine—until the divorce. Then things didn't seem to work out so well.

It is essential in the de-hiring process that the subordinate be isolated. To divide and conquer is the goal of the bosses. They must get the help of others on the staff. This is done through direct or implied orders to ignore and not support the person. This isolation can be manifested in several ways. In staff meetings our questions or comments are glossed over lightly; however, the same question from someone else is answered in detail. When we talk to the boss it is short, somber, and all business. Jobs that we have almost finished will be given to someone else, and then they get great praise for the total job well done; of course, something is wrong with us because we can never get a job done right.

I was observing a co-worker go through a de-hiring situation when I wrote "A Toast to a Ghost."

A Toast to a Ghost

In remembering
a number of cases,

I've been told
by those in high places,

If someone gets the ax
that you know,

Turn your head and pretend
you don't see them go.

For if you offer them
any support

Your tenure
will be short.

At this point I recognized I was seeing myself in someone else.

Then my own turn came to be de-hired, and I wrote "I Am Real!"

I Am Real!

Alone—
I sit among my peers,
they say I belong with them.

Yet I feel they don't see me,
as one does not see a mannequin.

They see me do my job
but as a warm mannequin
not a real person.

Those around me were not helping me; they'd either had direct orders or they feared that they would be next. But most of all I think they weren't helping me because most people only help those who will help themselves, and I was having trouble helping myself.

Are you helping yourself? Are you accepting help or are you running scared?

The stages of de-hiring

From our perspective as subordinates, de-hiring can happen in just three steps: step one, we trust the bosses, then they betray us; step two, credit for all of our good work is given to others; and then finally, they cut us to pieces with insults.

The letdown

Often the first step the bosses take in de-hiring is to tell us, "Trust us with your best interests," and then when we trust them, they let us down. Maybe we are not being let down deliberately or intentionally—maybe it's just that management has to be more concerned about the people who are performing the way they want them to perform and less concerned about those who are not. Take the merit raise: who gets the big raises, and who gets the little ones? If a storm blows up over the department's work: who is sheltered and reassured, and who is left out in the cold?

In retrospect, I was left discouraged with no monetary rewards and no shelter from the storms. Then I wrote "Trust Us" because I felt I had been betrayed.

Trust Us

They told me
when things go awry

Trust us
with your best interest.

But when the storm
had passed
And I could see
the wreckage,

Others had been shielded
from the storm
While I
floundered unnoticed.

I once worked for a boss who had an interesting but very irritating way of reviewing reports. He always wanted to see all drafts before the final typing. With some people, he would go over each draft in detail and make many very good suggestions. However, with others of us, he would give the drafts only a cursory glance. But when the report was published, he would pick it apart, pointing out how our work was always of inferior quality.

A friend told me of another kind of letting down. After he had made a major blunder because of an oversight, his supervisor told him that he was aware of the oversight before it was too late, but that he had chosen to say nothing to stop the blunder. I could not understand why he would deliberately let a person be hurt the way he had. After I got to know the supervisor, I realized he was that type of boss who is a Dr. Jekyll to those above him and a Mr. Hyde to those under him. In the eyes of top management, these bosses look good compared with people who make a few major blunders—some carefully planned.

If you feel you have been given job assignments and not been given the support to do them, you may be beyond the point where management judges you as a good worker. At this point you may have to consider seeking employment elsewhere, and you may need to get some help both to improve your self-image and to get a new job. You should consider whether you think your boss has let you down when you were trusting. You also need to consider how you felt and what caused the situation: were you really let down or was your boss just too overworked to notice you? Are you being oversensitive?

When the boss gives other people the credit for the work we have done, it may be unintentional or it could be a deliberate attempt to belittle us. From our point of view, the effect is usually the same. What may have happened is that the boss has simply stopped listening to us or we to the boss, but others on the staff are still listening; they take our ideas to the boss and the ideas are then accepted. Because the boss is not listening to us and we in effect no longer exist, a co-worker gets the credit and all the accolades. I remember sitting in a staff meeting and listening to a person get a lot of praise, and I wrote "Tarnished Halos."

Tarnished Halos

A ray of sunshine gleams
  from new polished gold
  and becomes a glint
  in the eye of those on high.

But from old gold
  worn with use
  and tarnished by age
  the sun reflects
  a muted soft tone.

It is this soft glow
  from old gold
  that forms a background
  against which
  the bright spots
  are contrasted.

But alas—
  the tarnished halos
  go unnoticed—
  to be forever lost
  among the discarded.

There are a number of ways to steal credit or to give it away. Some people seem to be prolific writers and have many publications in their names. Some have also used their writing skills to get promotions and then, as managers, they still seem to have the time for even more research and publishing. The catch is that some of these prolific writers do very little of their own original research. They work the system as follows: a person in the department does extensive research on a subject and publishes one or more articles, usually in obscure journals where few people in the field have a chance to read the results. The boss then writes a composite article, bringing together the staff member's work and related work by other researchers but mentioning that work only in footnoted references to the obscure journals. When colleagues read the article and all the references to the previous articles, our hero now looks like a great researcher.

Credit may go to the wrong people for other reasons.

One department head I knew had little professional experience related to the work he was overseeing and, as so often happens, he hired expert consultants. But because of his own lack of experience, he was unable to judge the quality of their work. To compound the problem, he was also under a lot of pressure to prove that his choices had been wise and that the consultants' work was of the highest quality. To prove this point, he would lavish praise on them, whatever they did. It was said that he even gave credit to his new "pet" group when other groups under him had done most of the work. Some people in the pet group would steal ideas and reports from the others and then blatantly publish the results under their own names. The department head apparently did nothing to stop this plagiarism. When faced by one of the real researchers and a consultant, his answer to the researcher's complaint was, "Why don't you two go someplace and settle this minor problem?"

Some bosses seem to encourage fighting among their subordinates. I know a schoolteacher who has worked for years in a school where people with "new" ideas were much praised by the principal. No credit was given for sharing ideas. The result was that teachers stole ideas from each other and called them their own. With credit only for new ideas and not for sharing, there began to develop a caste system among the teachers. As in any caste system, some of the teachers could gain a sense of self-worth only by discrediting the others. All the while the administration seemed either oblivious to what was going on, or positively supported it.

I think most people really believe in giving a fair day's work for a fair day's pay. But pay applies to more than just the paycheck. Often it is the lack of recognition for our special abilities that destroys our desire to give a fair day's work.

You should be concerned when you see your ideas going unheralded while someone else is getting all the credit for them. You should be concerned when you get more than your share of the assignments that have no challenge. If your boss doesn't seem to have time ever to say more than hello, you should consider how you feel and what caused the situation. Is it you, the boss, or circumstances beyond the control of either of you?

Insults hurt

The final step in de-hiring may be to belittle us with snubs and insults. These insults may be little things that didn't bothers us before or they may be very cutting. When we hear, "Someday you'll get a job right," we can laugh or we can feel insulted. How we feel will depend on how it is said and how we take it. I remember when my request for a job reclassification was rejected. I didn't mind the rejection so much as being told that how I felt was of no concern to the person making the decision. That prompted me to write "To Whom It May Concern."

To Whom It May Concern

When the cutting edge of insult
slashes deep
into the ego's tender heart,

It is the scab
woven from the fibers of fantasy
That binds and shields
the quivering wound
'til the scar
Born of realism
can fill the gaping void.

Then life can go on
almost as before.

De-hiring can create terrible pressures. I have seen a number of employees who were livid with anger because of the way they were being treated. I have read in the newspapers about employees who have physically injured their bosses. I know of one person who planned to hit the boss with a chair if he pushed any harder. In this case, the boss backed off, the crisis passed, and the employee was able to regain his control. I don't know whether that boss ever sensed how close he came to a serious situation.

Of course we all hear what we want to hear, and how we interpret what we hear depends to some extent on what we expect to hear. At times I think we are all somewhat like the

person who could never figure out how they trained that bird
to come out of the clock every hour on the hour and call
them names.

Periodically on the job we all feel the hurt of an insult
and we shrug and say, "Oh well." But if you seem to be
getting more than your share and the little ones seem to hurt
much more than they should, you may need to seek help in
finding out why you feel the way you do. Actions can be
louder insults than words. You may ask to go to a conference
but a junior colleague gets permission to go. You are told,
"Oh I forgot, maybe next time."

If you feel a lot of insults coming your way, consider
whether you are really a target or just oversensitive to tactless
remarks. It is the intent of the remarks that you must
evaluate: is the boss really trying to say "Why don't you go
away?"

On being transferred

Most organizations recognize that unhappy employees are not
very good workers, but that it is often much cheaper to try to
make an employee happy about the job than to hire a new
employee. Often the bosses will decide to move a troubled
individual to a different boss. The new boss may be able to
"straighten out" the employee. Often if we are not performing
as well as we should, we really know that something is wrong
and we may feel that the boss is out to get us. Because of
this, the bosses may not ask if we would like to move. We are
just told that we are being moved.

But sometimes you may have more power than you think
when a transfer seems inevitable. A lateral move is often
possible, and if you ask for the move before it is suggested,
you will feel better. Even if a transfer is downward, that is
not always a bad thing. I know a department head who
requested a move down in his own department. He made less
money but said he had a lot less stress. He told me he had
not liked the view from the top.

There are other ways of transferring. You may be able to
take on a special project that will give you fresh feelings of

self-worth. It might even bring you a pay raise or a bonus. You may want to take on job-enrichment tasks as special projects or as a means of gaining more autonomy. But such an arrangement often needs to be coupled with reinforced feedback. On one job I took on a job enrichment activity with my boss's blessing. I gained autonomy, but I did not realize until it was too late that my boss did not like the direction of my new activities. When I did get his feedback, it was a dark day and it heralded some very stormy times.

Transfers upward are not unknown. Sometimes a top manager will take care of a buddy that way. The promotion may be from "supervision" to "staff." I know two people who had such transfers at the same time. One eventually became a vice-president while the other disappeared into a dead-end job.

There are some managers who pride themselves on their lack of human compassion. They believe that any sign of concern for how people feel is a mark of an ineffective manager. I know of a manager like this who did not like the way one of the groups in his department was being run. Their work was adequate, so he had no real ground to fire them. Instead, he simply arranged that the complete function be transferred to a different department. In a subsequent general staff reshuffle, the function was dropped entirely. Then the original department head hired some new people who were promptly assigned the type of work done by the original group.

When we are transferred the boss may or may not be honest with us about the reasons. However, if we suspect that we are being moved because of our job performance, we may be able to find out who made the decision and ask if it was based on giving us a better chance to improve our performance. If we ask the question in a positive way, we may be able to get a straight answer. However, whether the bosses are right or wrong from our point of view, we cannot change their opinion by arguing that they are wrong. If we want to prove that they were wrong, we must make our job performance outstanding to overcome the low ratings we have had in the minds of our bosses.

If I ever reach the point again where I can't improve my

bad performance on the job and can't even think of anything that I can do well, I will know for sure that I need help. I will seek counseling for both my mental health and career planning. I would also seek help if I found myself again in a situation where I thought I was being de-hired. Otherwise, the slow torture of being de-hired might turn into the sudden shock of being fired.

Coming out on top
when the job ends

The end of the job, like the end of life itself, comes differently for different people. Some may know the end is near while others may never see it coming and then one day it is over. Or the end may come slowly and the person just fades into oblivion.

After the initial shock, the reaction to being fired can range from pleasure, to relief, to despondence. I heard someone say that the only reason he was unhappy was because he had been laid off before he could tell them to "take this job and shove it." In contrast was the department head in a large organization whose salary was frozen for several years before he was finally let go. He said that he should have quit years earlier because he will never be able to make up for those years when neither his salary nor his professional worth could grow.

We read in the newspaper about fired employees who do something violent to "even the score" with their ex-boss. But most people are not violent; they just won't let go. One man I know had reached retirement age when he was laid off. The organization had a service for helping such people find new jobs. He used the service and sent job applications all over the country, but stated in them that he would not move to another location. Somehow he needed to prove that he could not get a job before he could justify his decision to retire.

For some, the forced end of a job is exciting because it forces new opportunities and growth. For others, it is a relief because it relieves an oppressive pressure. But for some it can be a serious trauma. How we respond to the end of a job will depend on how we see ourselves. In this chapter I am talking mainly about those who are despondent at the end of a job.

If we are on the bottom end of the scale where we have lost appreciation for our personal worth, getting fired may be a very painful experience. We may not only feel that we have failed but we may tend to feel worthless, angry, hurt, and in general just feel bad. At the age of fourteen I was fired from my summer job at a nursery. I can still remember walking down the road muttering to myself about how unfair the boss had been. I know from today's perspective he was probably not at all unfair, but I only remember how much it hurt.

For all of us who have been despondent when the end of a job came, I wrote "Go Away."

Go Away

Too choked up to answer—
I heard them say:
old man why don't you go away.

You've been here a good many years
but there's a better place for you
out there somewhere.

Too stunned to really comprehend
too choked up to speak
too proud to cry
I sat mute—and
just shook my head
in disbelief.

They could not hear me say—
With all its faults
I love this place,
it's been like a second home.

But what I really meant was—
if I've failed here,
I'm scared to go out there.

Listening to our bodies and our bosses

Our employment health, like our physical health, will sometimes give us advance warning of impending doom. Both our bodies and our bosses will often give us signs that things are not as they should be. Our body is trying to tell us something when at the top of the stairs we are huffing and puffing with heart pounding, while someone else shows no sign of fatigue. The same is true of our days at work. If Friday finds us exhausted to the core but a co-worker suggests a game of tennis, that should tell us something about our work week. Why do we need the weekend to recover for that dreaded Monday morning while others have the energy to play all weekend? They come to work Monday morning for a chance to rest after a rousing weekend of fun and strenuous relaxation. Is your body trying to tell you something?

When we talk to our boss it is all business, but we hear laughter when others are talking to the boss. Do you overhear the boss giving praise to others but it has been a long time since you have heard any praise for your work? Is the boss telling you something?

Since we may not want to hear the messages from the body or the boss, we might find it very hard to listen. And when we do listen, it is often hard to believe the messages we hear.

I know a man whose moods and behavior on the job became so erratic that he was fired. He then turned morose and his behavior became so paranoiac that he was committed for psychiatric help. The first thing the hospital did was to give him a complete physical examination. It indicated that he had had a series of small strokes, and his change in behavior was directly attributable to that medical problem. Had he received the complete examination early enough, some of his problems may have been avoided.

It is very important to listen to our bodies as well as our bosses. Problems on the job can be directly related to medical problems.

Recovery means not giving up on ourselves

If you feel as I did when I wrote "The Time Has Come," then the time has come for you to go.

The Time Has Come

As I remember in years gone by
my boss always said
that my work was good.

But then came the sudden change,
a new job and a new boss.

Now I sit a little stunned
as my boss tells me
how I've done.

All the little errors
now look so big
and all I did well
is of little worth.

The time has come for me to go
but where I do not know.

If you are being fired, you will hear people saying that being fired was one of the best things that ever happened to them. And this may be true. Like having your wisdom teeth pulled, it may be the best thing to do but it still hurts like hell when it happens.

If you are an oldtimer, you may be given a long time to find a new job. If you are not, you may be given two weeks' pay in lieu of notice. In this case the first you may know about being fired is when you are told to go to Personnel and pick up your paycheck. Many organizations give two weeks pay in lieu of notice because the bosses know full well that you may do more harm than good during your last two weeks.

It may be helpful to write down how you are feeling. You may get out some hurts or anger by writing about your feelings, and it is very important to get as much of the anger and hurt feelings out of your system as soon as possible. You may lie about your feelings, but it is much better to be honest about them. It is okay to write, "I hate that s.o.b.'s guts." You may get the fastest relief by seeing a counselor. You should *not* go see your favorite bartender. There are already too many cases where a mixture of alcohol and anger have led to a tragic situation.

The important thing is not to give up on you, to get yourself back together again. You may well have thoughts of self-destruction. I did when I wrote "Numbered Days."

Numbered Days

Now in my final
  numbered days
Few speak—and none
  ask for advice.

My time is spent
  on trivial tasks
And running errands
  for secretaries.

I study the newspaper—
  looking for help wanted ads
  to match my resume.

And reading articles
  with more than a
  casual interest
  on how people
  commit suicide.

And for the first time
  I pray—for a
  quick heart attack.

Whenever you feel like this it is important to seek counseling. Above all else, it is important not to give up on yourself. You are the only one who really must keep your faith in you.

What has happened to those who gave up?

From the little towns to large cities, there are those who have given up. Many are recluses hidden away in little rooms, out of sight and out of mind. They have lost track of their loved ones and no one knows who they are. They just hide away. Many are not old—at least in years.

There are others whom we have all known. They do not hide in little rooms but they hide inside their minds, often blocking away the outside world with wine and drugs. They hide inside a hardened, self-imposed shell composed largely of bitterness. I know a man who for months would talk about his ex-boss with his fists clenched and hatred in his voice. In a year of unemployment he seemed to age ten years. He was a bitter and frightened man obsessed with the hurts of the past. Another man I know always seemed to feel as if management were out to get him. When he was informed about the possibility that he could be affected by a reduction in the work force, he went into a rage about how unfair the system had been to him. He was transferred and not laid off, but he remained certain that the transfer was just a management technique to get him to quit.

Others who give up are overwhelmed by loneliness, despair, and remorse. For all of these people I wrote "The Lonely Old Man." The feelings are the same whether the person is old or young, male or female.

The Lonely Old Man

The cold wind cuts
through the old man's coat
As he shivers in line
for a bowl of soup.

He will sleep tonight
but he knows not where
But he does know
that nobody will care.

You have the keys to your own prison

The people who have given up on themselves have built the strongest prison in the world. Then they've gone inside and thrown away the key. Since you are reading this, you still have a key in your hand. Don't throw it away because no one can pick the lock to your prison. If as you are reading you feel you have already built your prison and are part way in, don't slam the door! Get out and tear down those prison walls. You must take some positive steps to escape from your own prison.

First, look at yourself in the mirror and say out loud, "I need help." There's nothing wrong with saying that. If you broke your leg you would call for help. This time it is your self-respect that is broken, so call for help just the same. Tell your loved ones that you need help. They may be able to help you an amazing amount on their own and can at least help you find the best type of specialist. The next step is to go to the specialist and get the help you need.

Specialists can only help if you help yourself. They can only give advice; you are the one who must follow the advice. If you do, you can soon walk again with your head held high and a spring in your step.

You will start looking for a new job. But the most important look is at yourself. You need to look at the things you do, your abilities, and your skills. You may have spent years in the wrong job. You may have started in the job for any of a number of reasons, but at this point you are not doing your job very well. You may have begun to lose faith in your own ability to do any job well.

Unfortunately at this point you may feel others are telling you that you are no damn good, your skills are useless, you are less than adequate as a person. I know I found myself with a master's degree looking at help wanted ads for custodians. When I realized what I was doing, it came as a real shock to learn how far my self-confidence had slipped.

The important thing is to look realistically at our skills and abilities. We shouldn't look at how we have performed when we were not working very well, but instead at the times when we did do our job well.

To go up you must look up and not down. Most important, you need to look at yourself and answer the questions: Who am I? What do I like to do? To feel good about yourself you must start to say, "I'm okay." If you can't say, "I'm great," at least say, "I'm adequate."

A few years of despair and lessening self-respect is a living hell for the person, the loved ones, and all who know them. I doubt that many marriages could last through more than one of these experiences. Many people have been to the bottom of the well and have gotten out, and have never gone down again. Once to the bottom was enough. Others can help but we must do the climbing.

If you feel you are at the end of your rope, tie a knot and hang on—rest for a while, and then start climbing.

The next section of this book is designed to help you make that climb quickly and keep you from ever falling back into despair about your job, your boss, or you.

PART TWO

Coming up to job success

Your skills and interests

As far as the employment part of our lives is concerned, there are basically only three things that we can change: our jobs, our bosses, and ourselves. In each case we have some choices. We can keep doing the same work we are doing now, or we can make a job or career change. We can change our relationships with our bosses, or change bosses by changing jobs. We can look in the mirror each morning at the same person, or we can get to know ourselves a little better.

Mid-life career changes have become acceptable, and many people change careers several times during their working lifetimes.

There are some people in their 90's who continue to be excited about their productive activities. In a retirement home that I visit, there is a pert lady of 105 and many lively people in the 80's, including a pair of newlyweds. My mother at 84 went back to college to start a new career as a writer. We then gave her the new typewriter she requested for her 85th birthday. Her first book was published by the college when she was 86. She has started her second book and has plans to do many more.

In the world of employment, there is a general trend toward more job flexibility. Currently about one-fifth of all adult Americans are working part-time. Some of these people, men as well as women, devote the rest of their time to raising children or other activities that bring no cash reward. Others try to start their own small businesses. We are only "stuck" where we are by default. At any age or level of skill, we can change our work some way or another. However, considering a change and making a change are two different things. To make a change in a job or career may involve a lot of effort, money, and stress.

I know I have feared changing my work in any way and would tell myself that it really didn't matter. But it did matter, for I ran the risk of sinking into a deeper depression. It has been said that, from a psychological point of view, the safest place in the world is to be in a state of mild depression. If we can maintain this state, we do not risk failure in going either up or down. But no condition is static—we are bound to go up or down whether we like it or not. So regardless of what anyone else says, you must take the responsibility and the risk of saying that your work life, like the whole of your life, really does matter.

If a change is what you think you need, you need to make the decision on the best information you can get. Don't change (or stay put) out of ignorance, self-pity, or fear. You are important.

A good way to start making a job or career decision is to look at yourself and decide what you really like to do.

Skills you like to use

We all have a set of skills that we like to use whenever we can, and on the job we try to use them whether they are appropriate or not. These are the activities that we enjoy doing and we are often proud of the results when we can freely use these skills. Our preferred skills are very satisfying to us, and when we cannot use them we may become frustrated.

As an example of what two different people like to do, I can compare myself and a colleague. I am always looking for new ways to do things and I enjoy figuring out how things work. I am not very good at finishing jobs because as soon as I know how something works, I tend to lose interest. On the other hand, my co-worker does not like to figure out how things work but accepts them as they are. She prefers a neat work area, with a place for everything and everything in its place. In this respect we are completely different—neither of us better than the other, but just different. The things I am good at and like to do are best suited for a job that requires new ideas. My co-worker is good at and likes to keep records, making sure all of the details are taken care of. We could not have the same type of work and both be happy with it.

Our preferred skills, when defined in basic terms, seem to remain the same throughout our lives. We use these preferred skills over and over again, never seeming to tire of exercising them. Our enjoyment in using them is almost insatiable. Once we find out what we really like to do, what gets us excited, we can then see how we can use these preferred skills to our advantage to control how we do our jobs.

I helped identify my preferred skills by listing many activities that I enjoyed doing, did well, and was proud of. This list was based on fond memories from all ages and all parts of my life. The list included figuring out how something worked, building a new model, working as a youth leader, taking the kids to the zoo, inventing a new way of doing a routine chore. I wrote down whatever came to mind. I found that writing about myself was a lot easier when I could find a place where I would not be interrupted, a quiet and peaceful place where I could just relax and let my memory fly back to the exciting times in my life. In such a place I could laugh out loud at a funny time, or just smile one of those big smiles when I remembered with pride something well done.

You may want to remember some of your proud moments, and jot down what you were proud of. Just ignore

what anyone else said or would say about those occasions.
Recall them if for no other reason than the pure joy of
remembering.

There may be several things we may be good at doing
but we don't necessarily get a big kick out of doing. They may
not be deadly dull but they sure are not very exciting. For
me, I enjoy setting up a system for doing something and I can
keep the system going, after a fashion, but I am not really
interested in keeping it going. Of course, there are also
activities that we don't enjoy doing and are also not at all
good at.

It would be great to get paid well for a job that is made
up of just the exciting things we really like to do.
Unfortunately, many jobs consist of all three kinds of
activities—a little of the exciting work that we sometimes do
too well, a lot of the so-so work that we can do well enough,
and some that we don't like and don't do very well.

Most people end up with work some place between the
two extremes. But there are people who spend most of their
time, avocation and vocation, on the types of activities that
they are excited about. They live very exciting lives. There
are other people who put up with forty hours a week on a
barely tolerable job just so they can get a paycheck and then
go away from work to do their exciting activities—or possibly
nothing at all.

Try some simple solutions to complex problems

We are very complex people, living in a very complex world,
and confronted with very complex problems. It has often
been said that when people offer a simple explanation to a
complex problem, they don't understand the problem. I
disagree. I believe that a simple explanation can give us a
clearer overview, and then we can see when, how, and if we
need to use complex solutions. I remember an address by Dr.
Edward Teller, the nuclear physicist. Most of his audience
were scientists and engineers. He responded to a long and

complex question with words to the effect that: I am not sure I understand what you meant by what you just said, but if you can't explain it briefly in simple terms, then you don't understand it either.

To those that continue to say that only simple people come up with simple explanations, I say, "$E = MC^2$ to you."

So with that, I go into a simple overview of the types of activities that can be exciting to different people. This is a "Preference Profile." Developing it and testing it out on my friends were activities that I found very exciting. It was designed to give an overview of what we prefer doing. This Preference Profile, like many of my other suggestions, is not exhaustive—or exhausting. It is presented here to help get you started in the right direction. After all, the quest for more exciting work is yours. I can only suggest where you may look for treasure maps. I can't tell you for sure where they are, what is on them, or even what the treasures may be.

For the millions of people doing a wide variety of activities, exciting or dull, I have had the audacity to lump all their interests into just four general categories: people and things, order and change. I will admit that using just four categories produces a very general overview. However, this simple approach does give a first-order approximation of what we truly like or dislike doing.

Using just four categories makes it easier to see the similarity between different activities. For example, there is my friend, a scientific researcher, who likes to play bridge and is a very good player. He is also a merit-badge counselor for the Boy Scouts. He has a reputation at work for being tough but fair—the information in a report must be right and so must the spelling. He will take all the time needed with the boys, and the report must be exactly right before he will approve it. There is one single characteristic that is common to all of these activities and attitudes. My friend likes things to be in order. I don't ever remember talking with him when he didn't emphasize the importance of order. Order seems to dominate his life. He thinks about change only to the extent that it will help put things and information in order.

He talks about people in terms of them doing things in the proper way.

I know another man who is very proud of what he calls his intuitive abilities. He says he is very sensitive to the feelings of people and can sense when they are about to do something. He is also very dominated by order. He is aware of the social structure of the organization, the pecking order, and it is very important to him that everyone do what is required according to their status in the organization. How people feel is much less important than how they fit in. He is dominated by people and order, and change is acceptable only if it helps put people in their place.

Even though both of these men like order, one thinks mainly about things and the other mainly about people, so they would probably have very little of interest to talk to each other about. Knowing these two real people, I can't conceive of them ever reaching agreement on anything.

I have often heard people from the engineering side of an organization say that there is no one in the personnel office whom they can really talk to. "They are a bunch of touchy-feelies way out in left field." Of course, personnel people look at engineering as "cold and insensitive to the real needs of people; in need of learning how to be sensitive and to communicate better." I am sure that when a psychologist talks to his accountant about income tax, the discussion is a strain for both of them. The psychologist may mutter, "He doesn't seem to know that there are things more important than numbers. I know my checks won't bounce; I checked my balance a few months ago."

The Preference Profile can help us identify what we like to do, what our job requires us to do, and what our dream job would be like. At a later stage, career planning can show us how to get where we want to go once we know where we want to go.

At this point you may find a number of books to be of value; there are several that I have found interesting.

Richard Bolles has published several books, but two of these may be of specific value at this point in your personal growth. They are *What Color is Your Parachute? A Practical*

Manual For Job-Hunters and Career-Changers* and *The Three Boxes of Life and How To Get Out of Them.***

There is also a new book entitled *Growing: A Woman's Guide to Career Satisfaction†* by Burack, Albrecht, and Seitler. Men should not be turned off by the title: it is equally as good for men as it is for women. I found the book interesting because it is a good guide to increasing career satisfaction. I also gained an insight into the world of women.

These and other books are listed in the bibliography.

Describing what you like to do with a Preference Profile

Like a sentence, our lives are made up of subjects and verbs. The subjects are generally either things or people. The verbs are activities that generally establish order or make changes with these things or people.

How often we think in each of these areas will depend on our broad interests. We can rate our interest in people, things, order, and change from a low of dislike, to seldom, sometimes, frequent, or to a high of dominate:

| 0,1 | 2,3 | 4,5,6 | 7,8 | 9,10 |
| Dislike | Seldom | Sometimes | Frequent | Dominate |

This rating, of course, is not exact but is a first-order approximation.

The general levels of interest can be described as follows:

DISLIKE: We avoid thinking about the subject and we will walk away from discussions about it; the thought of it almost makes us ill.

SELDOM: It seldom occurs to us to think about the subject.

*Berkeley, CA: Ten Speed Press, rev. 1978.
**Berkeley, CA: Ten Speed Press, 1978.
†Belmont, CA: Lifetime Learning Publications, 1980.

SOMETIMES: When we need to, we think about the subject.

FREQUENT: We think about other things but we frequently think about the subject.

DOMINATE: Interest in this area dominates our lives; we go to extremes to be involved in this area of interest.

I have known people who so disliked machines that they would go hungry before they would put a coin into a food-vending machine. I have known others at work who so disliked thinking about people and feelings that they would almost hide in their offices. I have also known some people who were completely dominated by either things or people. But most of us would probably rate ourselves somewhere between 3 and 7 in all of the four areas.

Your interest in people

I use the heading "people" to cover all of the feeling aspects of life. This means thinking about people as human beings, not as tools or warm robots that are essentially things.

Those of us interested in people often enjoy reading psychology books, novels, or love stories. We watch TV or movies where the characters develop strong relationships. We are sensitive to the feelings of those around us. We enjoy trying to figure out what is going on inside the minds of other persons—what they are feeling—and then we often feel a sense of pride when our predictions come out right. When we are in a meeting where the subject is not of vital interest to us, we like to watch the group in action and figure out who is going to assume which role. We take pride in not being surprised by other people's reactions.

I frequently think about people's feelings and so I rate my interest in people at about 7. Rate yourself on the people interest scale:

PEOPLE

0						*ME*			10
0,1		2,3		4,5,6		7,8		9,10	
Dislike		Seldom		Sometimes		Frequent		Dominate	

Your interest in things

People who think about things envision the relationships between things. They have many ideas about the physical world—real or imagined. People are sometimes considered things, that is, warm robots. Henry Ford is quoted as saying, "My job is to pay them. Their job is to work. So what is all the fuss about?"

Those of us who like to think about things enjoy figuring out how they work; we may even lie awake nights wondering why something won't work. We have a workshop or lab at home and we enjoy reading engineering or technical materials. We take pride in the things in our lives—a camera, a violin, a car, or tools—and what we can do with them. We may think of new and better ways to use the things we think about. We may have a high or a low interest in people's feelings; if it is low, we may even react to a person as we would to a squeaking robot that is out of adjustment.

I rate myself at about 7 on the things scale because I frequently am interested in things. Rate yourself on the scale. Mark "dominate" if thoughts about things dominate your life; mark "dislike" if the thought of using a machine makes you ill.

THINGS

0,1	2,3	4,5,6	7,8	9,10
Dislike	Seldom	Sometimes	Frequent	Dominate

Your interest in order

Order and change underlie the activities we do with both people and things.

Those who like order often say, "A place for everything and everything in its place." They may believe there is only one right way to do anything, and that is the way it must be done. They like procedures that tell them what they are supposed to do: they read cookbooks and cook by the book; their checkbooks balance and they pay their bills on time. They like a very predictable world, no clutter; the house is clean and so is their desk. There is no miscellaneous category in their files. They will practice until they get it right. They like change only if it is to make things right. They like to put things together and feel good when all the pieces fit. They easily remember all the rules and patterns: they take great pride in being able to quote a rule, a procedure, or any authority. They enjoy knowing where things and people belong and what they should do.

My kids gave me a sign for my office which reads "A Clean Desk Is The Sign Of A Sick Mind." I don't really believe it even though my desk is often messy. There is nothing wrong with liking order—although there can be some problems when a "pack rat" and a "neat freak" are married to each other.

As for me, I rate myself as a "seldom" when it comes to order—about 2. I'll never be known as a "neat freak," I'm a little messy, and I dislike balancing my checkbook and keeping records.

Rate yourself from 0 to 10 somewhere on the order scale. If you are always putting things, people, your whole life in the right order, mark 9 or 10. Mark 0 or 1 if having to put things in order or follow a set procedure makes you ill.

ORDER

0,1	2,3	4,5,6	7,8	9,10
Dislike	Seldom	Sometimes	Frequent	Dominate

Your interest in change

Change includes both changing people and changing things.

Persons who like change, and I am one of them, like to think about having things different from how they are now, about trying new ways of doing anything. We think about how people can change, how things can be changed, how to change ideas and concepts, about new relationships between things, concepts, and people. We may say, "The status quo has got to go; if it is up to me, a change you'll see." Just for the fun of it we think about inventions, creating new ways of doing something. We like to take the tried and true and compare it with many other ways to see if something is better. If the boss starts to tell a creative person how to do something, before the explanation is halfway through that person can often see many other ways to do the job. Creative cooks seldom follow a recipe, creative musicians often like to improvise, creative managers find new and exciting ways to apply people's talents.

My wife put a sign on my study door which reads, "A Creative Mess Is Better Than Tidy Idleness," and that describes me fairly well. I am not sure if one can have tidy creativity. On the change scale I rate myself very close to a "dominate," maybe at 9. If you love change, mark 9 or 10; if changes in people or things or ideas distress you, mark 0 or 1.

CHANGE

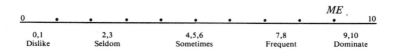

0,1	2,3	4,5,6	7,8	9,10
Dislike	Seldom	Sometimes	Frequent	Dominate

There is nothing "wrong" with any preference rating for people, things, order, and change. All of us are different but not wrong. The important question is how well our particular likes and dislikes fit our jobs.

Why some jobs feel right and some do not

When we analyze how a person and a job fit, we must *not* look at two very important considerations: how to get a job and the pay. These two subjects are covered later.

Rating ourselves on each of the four scales—people, things, order, and change—is a good place to start evaluating our job fit. As an example, let's look at what artists do and why many artists don't enjoy being commercial artists.

Consider first an amateur artist who works hard at his own painting and really appreciates other people's works. However, his present job is unrelated to art. The question is, should he become a commercial artist?

Let's assume for our example that there is a job opening for a product illustrator, someone to make artistic renditions of products. Now let's look at the job requirements as they would appear on the four Preference Profile scales:

PEOPLE: **Seldom** needs to think much about how people will interact with each other.

THINGS: **Frequent** interest in using the art media.

ORDER: **Frequent** need to make renditions that look like the original. There is little latitude; the renditions must match the engineering drawings.

CHANGE: **Seldom** needs to think about new ways to do the renditions.

Is this a good job for the amateur artist? To find out, let's look at what this artist likes to do. He likes to make paintings that look like photos, and likes to work from photographs or engineering drawings. He uses the same media all the time and likes to work all alone in his studio. His Preference Profile would be:

SCALES	JOB	ARTIST #1
PEOPLE	Seldom	Seldom
THINGS	Frequent	Frequent
ORDER	Frequent	Frequent
CHANGE	Seldom	Seldom

This is a good job fit. He would probably love every minute of the commercial art job.

Now let's look at a different artist. She does abstract painting, uses a wide variety of media, and will try anything that is new. In her works she tries to capture the essence of how she feels about experiences she has had with other people. This artist has the following Preference Profile:

SCALES	JOB	ARTIST #2
PEOPLE	Seldom	Frequent
THINGS	Frequent	Seldom
ORDER	Frequent	Seldom
CHANGE	Seldom	Frequent

Is this a good job for this artist? No! She would go out of her mind and so would her boss. She would likely hate every minute of every working day.

Contrasting Preference Profiles can be shown in most career fields. The musicians who practice until they get a Beethoven symphony absolutely correct and the New Orleans jazz musicians who fill the air with improvisations will have contrasting Preference Profiles. Every individual and every specific job may have a different Preference Profile. But the closer the job's and person's profiles match, the more worthwhile and exciting the job will be for that person.

Checking your Preference Profile

Now that you know how you can use the Preference Profile rating, you may want to think again about the "subjects" and "verbs" that have been exciting in your life and whether they support the way you rated yourself. For example, my Preference Profile is as follows:

PEOPLE: Frequent—I rated myself as a 7 because I like to be around people and I am filled with joy when babies are born, when people marry, when they have birthdays. I cry at happy times and I also choke up when people are hurt.

THINGS: Frequent—I rated myself about a 7 because I also always like to think about things, about rebuilding or changing everything I see. I want to know what makes everything "tick."

ORDER: Seldom—I rated myself at 3 because I often don't put things in order, I dislike balancing the checkbook, and my office is sometimes a mess. But I do coordinate the colors of my clothes and I like my social life to be orderly.

CHANGE: Dominate—I rated myself as a 9 because I like to think about changing everything around me. However, I like to keep the same people around me—but I do like for them to grow as persons.

Making sure you get the right answers

If you have written some notes or lists about your job, your boss and yourself, go back and read what you have written and look for wrong answers. Any kind of a personal profile can have wrong answers. The answers are wrong if they do not honestly reflect how you feel or do not give an accurate description of you. A rating on your Preference Profile is correct only if it describes *you* the way *you* know *you* are and not the way someone else wants you to be.

The idea of lying to ourselves is not new. Louis Pasteur said in 1876, "The greatest derangement of the mind is to believe in something because we wish it to be so." If you have described someone else, the person you would like to be, go back and correct it. Don't lie to yourself. Throughout our lives we have been told by our parents, teachers, bosses, advertisers, spouses, and even our children what we *should* be like. It is hard to separate what we have been told we want and like from what we really want and like. Your Preference Profile is about you and is for you. So be as honest as possible with yourself.

The requirements of your current job

To get a comparison of your own Preference Profile and your job's Preference Profile, you can take your current job—or the one you've just lost—and list what it requires of you. To do this, it may help to divide the job into big chunks, the major different types of activities. In all our jobs there are parts that we don't like to do, and hopefully these take only a small amount of our time and energy. If an error in these activities will not get us fired or get the boss in trouble, then we can take the bitter with the sweet and regard these tasks as minor.

I rate my job as an industrial training specialist about as follows:

PEOPLE: I need to be interested in people but not to

the point that it clouds my judgment. I need to think sometimes about people's feelings:

THINGS: I work in technical training so I frequently need to be interested in and have an understanding of things.

ORDER: I need to make sure that all of the course records are kept in good order. I also need to be concerned about keeping all of the training materials in good order. Order does not dominate my job but it is sometimes required, so I rate my job a 6.

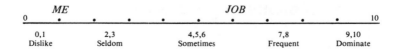

CHANGE: In all training programs we are concerned about people changing the way they do tasks, but we are not necessarily concerned with new ways to use things. I frequently have to think about ways people and things change, so I rate my job at 7.

Plotting personal and job Preference Profiles

After you have rated your job in terms of its requirements or "preferences," compare it with your own Preference Profile. To do this, plot them on the same scales as shown below.

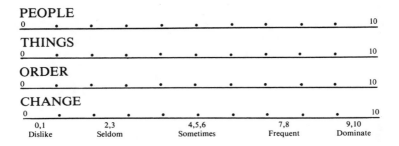

PEOPLE and THINGS are basically opposite physical entities, and ORDER and CHANGE are opposite activities. Thus the four categories can be plotted on scales numbered from opposite ends and then placed at right angles to form a graph:

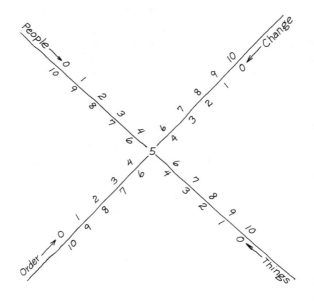

To use this Preference Profile graph, just plot your ratings and then draw a line between the points on the scales—People, Change, Things, Order—and then back to People. This is a plot of my Preference Profile and my job's Preference Profile:

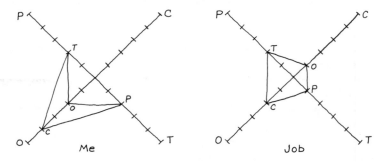

Plotting each major different part of your job may help you consider how you could reorganize your work to make it fit your personal Preference Profile better. For example, if I had to be a lot less concerned about order and a little more concerned about people's feelings, and about changing people or things, I would have a much better job fit. In fact, I tend not to keep things in order and I spend too much time on the human side of my job; that is, I do my work more according to my Preference Profile than to my job's Preference Profile. I keep trying to change my job gradually to match my interests better.

By comparing your personal and your job Preference Profiles with those of your co-workers, you may be able to do some swapping and all of you may be a lot happier. There may be parts of your job that you dislike but they may be the activities that someone else is very envious of because you get to do them all the time.

On the following page is a plot of the two artists and the commercial art job.

Artist number one seems a natural for the job and artist number two would probably never fit in. As artists, they might find very little to talk about. People whose preference profiles have some similarity often find many more subjects of common interest.

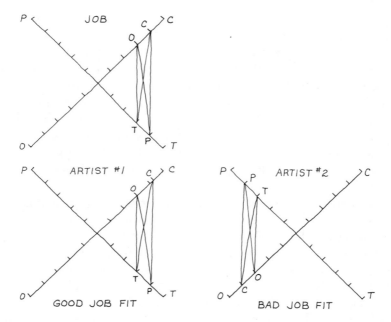

Should you change jobs or stay put?

Why change jobs? I think we have all known people who have changed jobs or careers and have regretted it. They talk about the job they gave up and say that it was much better than their current job. I know at times I have had fears of changing jobs because I did not know what the other job might really be like. I think we have also known people who have changed jobs often but never gone up the ladder, gotten more money, or even more job satisfaction. They may still be hunting for that perfect job, but they may not recognize it when they see it.

We should change jobs or careers only for a reason, we should know the reason, and we should be honest with ourselves. Of course, the same is true of staying put: we should stay for a reason and know the reason.

I have changed jobs and stayed put for the wrong reasons. I changed careers because I felt it was better to be "professional," and I stayed put in a job because of a fear of the unknown and a loss of a positive self-image. I can vividly remember the reasons I gave myself. I thought I could stay on the job and prove myself. But I really know that a boss convinced of my worth against his will is still a boss convinced against his will. There was in reality no way that this boss would ever understand the way I looked at my work, nor would I ever understand his way. I was lying to myself and I knew it, but at the time I would not admit it. Never underestimate the importance of being honest with yourself, your spouse, your friends, your kids, and maybe even your boss.

A friend told me about a co-worker who was a lackluster man, the sort who does the work but without much enthusiasm. Then one day my friend met this man at a meeting of a model powerboat club. He was in charge of the meeting and busy helping people solve their equipment problems. He seemed to be a different person and was having a great time. Now he was bright, articulate, and very enthusiastic about what he was doing. It was the same person but in a very different type of activity.

Really enjoying our jobs can make a big difference in our lives. At least some part of each day's work should be exciting to us. If it is not, our bosses may see only a ho-hum, so-so employee and never know the real us who finds life exciting and worth living.

I know a woman who has been doing the same type of work for over ten years. I commented to her that she must enjoy her work because she has been doing it so long. She simply said, "I do what I am paid to do, but that does not mean that I enjoy the work." It seems sad to me that this person has spent perhaps twenty thousand hours of her life doing a job that she does not really enjoy. Come to think of it, I have probably done the same over the last thirty years. I guess I have spent a third of my working life on activities I did not enjoy.

Why do we do jobs we don't enjoy? There are some very good reasons. Money comes high on the list. Most of us worked at whatever we could just for money when going through school. But we were young and it was all so new and exciting, we could put up with a ho-hum job because it was short term and helped us get what we really wanted in the long term. We could put up with almost anything. But now circumstances are different.

Another reason we stay put is that we feel we are too far into a retirement system to get out. With a family, we may stay for the security or we may feel that we are too highly specialized to get a job anyplace else. We may also stay on a job because we like where we live. Many people pick the place they want to live and take any job they can to support them.

At least know the reason you have stayed put. If you feel you have stayed put too long, you may find it helpful to write down your reasons and analyze them carefully.

Looking at greener pastures

I will always remember seeing two flocks of sheep with a fence between them. Every sheep on both sides of the fence had its head through the fence, each eating grass on the other side.

I guess there are times when we all long for greener pastures. We long for the kind of job a friend has because it pays so much better than ours, or is more interesting, or has some other strong attraction. It may be that we are just tired of the same boss, the same work, the same everything, and just want a change.

There is another very real reason why some people may be unhappy in their jobs. They may have too much talent for the job, or a specific gift that makes their job a burden. In a music appreciation class, I sat next to a woman as we listened to recordings of classical music played by great artists. I enjoyed the music but the woman often grimaced as we listened. She said later that she was both blessed and cursed with a perfect sense of pitch. There was almost no musical performance that she could enjoy, and a note that was a hair's breadth off caused her physical torment. I could imagine the tortures she would suffer if she were a music teacher in school.

It is important to look honestly at what we want, what we can do, and what our job is now. We then need to take a

close and honest look at our dream job. We should do a
Preference Profile on it and check it against our personal
Preference Profile. If the fit is good, we need to look very
closely at the negative side of that possible future job. We
need to look very hard because when we want something, we
tend to overlook its faults. Over the fence in that greener
pasture there are thistles—parts of that new job that will not
be to our liking. If you are after a dream job, write down all
of the negative things you can think about. For me, that
dream job might be photography, which is now a serious and
very satisfying hobby. Once I considered it as a possible
profession and at that time I met a man who worked as a
landscape photographer for a major greeting card company.
Since no one can live where there are unlimited landscapes,
he had to travel a lot. He was gone from home most of the
time; this week to the desert and next week to the mountains
and next month to the seashore. He had to produce a large
number of specific scenes each month. For me, doing
production landscape photography would have taken the fun
out of my hobby, and I would also not accept any job that
often took me away from my family.

However, it will be different after I retire. My wife and I
want to travel and I plan to do freelance landscape
photography. I will then be doing what I like and when I
like, and so it will be fun.

I have a friend who took a new job with good potential
for personal and financial growth. However, in less than a
month he quit and was out again looking for a job. In effect,
his personal Preference Profile and his new job's Preference
Profile were not a good match. The real people and the real
job were enough different from what he had expected that he
knew it would not work out. So he felt he had to quit.
Fortunately, much of the work that he had done to find that
job was still current and made his new job hunt easier.

Of course, now it is easy to say, "He should have . . . ."
But from his experience we can at least learn to look before
we leap. If we are looking seriously at a new job, we should
make sure that our decision is not unreasonably biased by our
desire to leave our current job. We must make decisions that
balance our emotions and our logic.

Will it be a job change
or a career change?

If you have decided the time has come to make a
change in your employment, the question is whether
to make a change in your job or in your career.
Making a career change means that you would be
doing something very different from your present job.
A job change would simply mean you will still be
doing the same type of work but for a different boss in
the same organization or in a different place.

As an example: I have a friend who was a head
nurse in an intensive care unit at a hospital. After
seven years she was finally burned out; she was
exhausted physically, emotionally, and mentally. She
had to make a change, so she quit. Fortunately, she
was able to work part-time and could keep food on the
table. She finally had to make a choice—stay in
nursing or get out and do something completely
different.

A job change would mean nursing but in a
different hospital, working in a doctor's office,

becoming an industrial nurse, school nurse, or any number of other options available in the nursing field. The first thing she had to do was decide what she liked to do. I know her as a very warm, caring, outgoing person who likes to help people. She said she enjoys combining her helping activities with her high technical skills as a nurse; in other words, she liked nursing as a career. With this decision clear, she then needed to find a new job in her chosen career field—a job where she could do nursing but not a job where she would again become overstressed and burn out.

Making career decisions

The job versus career decision is a tough decision and one that needs a lot of consideration.

In the musical "Chorus Line," a dancer is injured and the director asks all the other dancers to think about what they would do if they could never dance again.

I think that is a question we should all ask ourselves every once in awhile. It is easy to see how a dancer could be injured and never dance again. But how about you and me? Most of our jobs don't require great physical strength and agility, yet there may be many reasons we could no longer stay in our current career. An auto accident could affect any of us, physically or mentally, or unless we keep current our skills could become outdated. There are many good teachers who are not teaching now just because they cannot find a job in their profession. The supply and demand for almost every type of expertise seems to vary from time to time. A few years ago, there were many good people working in the slide rule business, but today they have joined the "has beens." A whole generation of graduating engineers may never have even seen a slide rule in use.

As for me, I have several choices if I could not find a job in industrial training. I have my teaching credentials so I may be able to do some substitute teaching. I also do some consulting and I have a part-time photography business. I could do some writing. I am somewhat skilled as a cabinetmaker and in related trades. I have kept my options open because I have faced the possibility of a career change.

Some of my skills are no longer really useful. Over twenty years ago I taught electronics. Then after I had been out of the field for about five years, I realized that my skills were no longer of value, and today I can't even understand the new textbooks. Nevertheless, my current skills leave me with several different career options, and I could get retraining to update some of my other skills.

I have a friend who was a scientist and had a good job. However, he liked to build things with his hands. So he started doing cabinetwork as a hobby and within a few years, he quit his job and went full-time into his own custom cabinet business.

Consider some of your own career possibilities. You may find that some of your options are far more interesting than your current job or the one you may be looking for.

Knowing what you like to do

I think many of us keep telling ourselves that we really enjoy what we're doing, but sometimes we lie to ourselves. We can tolerate the job, but we really don't look forward to going to work tomorrow morning. We can be tolerant of a job we don't really enjoy and sometimes even improve our job performance, if we are working toward one that we will enjoy. Or we may decide to tolerate our present job and spend the time and energy on a hobby. I once met a man who has a science Ph.D. and he also taught folk dancing as a paying hobby. I've heard recently that he has quit his job as a scientist and now teaches folk dancing for a living. He may not make as much money, but I would bet he is a much happier man. Of course, you may not be able to make a living at your hobby. But if you can tolerate your work and really enjoy your hobby, at least you are having some excitement in your life.

What do you get excited about doing, and would you really like to do it full-time? Look at your Preference Profile and think over some of the activities you like doing in each of the four areas: people, things, order, and change. Note as many different activities as you can think of; at this point, these do not have to be things that you are skilled at doing or that can ever get you a job, or that could make you enough money to live on even if you had a job doing them. We will get to these practical problems later. You are now just writing down all of the activities that you like to do.

As I wrote down what I liked to do, I could see me there in black and white. I was surprised at some items but when I showed my list to others, they agreed that it was a good representation of what I tended to do. For instance, I like to find new ways of doing things. The kids say that nothing ever came into our house without being modified. I enjoy electronics and photography because there are so many new things to learn. I enjoy helping foreign visitors with their spoken English because I learn about their countries and I also learn more about my mother tongue.

I think most of us change over the years. What may have been a thrill may now even be a bore. Be sure your list of likes reflects you as of now.

Know what you can do

After you have written down all the things you *like* to do, the next step is to identify which of them you do well or could learn to do well, ignoring still the matter of making a living.

Then think about your present career field and the skills that are needed by people who are really good in it.

You'll find that different jobs in your career field have different requirements. For example, schoolteachers vary widely in both their personal preference profiles and job requirements. Effective kindergarten teachers need to be very interested in children's feelings and the growth of each child as a person. Their interest in subject matter can be secondary. On the other hand, the good high school chemistry teacher needs to have a high interest in the subject but does not necessarily need to have a high interest in how each of the students feels. Of course, the best balance is a teacher who likes people and the subject. Unfortunately there are unhappy teachers who have high subject interests but teach in the primary grades where there is a greater need for human interest.

There are needs for people with all types of different

preference profiles. For instance, in a research and development organization it is necessary to have people who have a lot of fun dreaming up new ideas, who get all excited when they think of a new way to do something. As you listen to them talk about a new idea, they are like little kids with a new toy. And like a new toy, the idea does not have to do anything—it is just fun to play with. Without these creative people who are dominated by ideas of change, R&D organizations would eventually become ineffective.

However, once the new idea has been proposed, someone else may have to decide whether it is practical and usable enough to warrant development. This someone likes to think about new ideas but also likes to make sure that the new idea fits into the organization's needs. If it fits in, a third person should work over the new idea and make sure all of the details are right. This person needs to have a high interest in order, in testing and retesting the new idea to make sure it is absolutely right.

All three types of people will be doing what they like to do in this type of organization. However, if the people who come up with the new ideas have to carry them all the way through to the final development and field testing, they may dislike that part of their jobs. On the other hand, if the persons who like order are required to come up with new and creative ideas and ways to make changes, they too may not like part of their jobs.

What happens when jobs don't fit?

What I believe has happened in many lagging R&D organizations is that creative people who have fun with new ideas are now supervised by people who like order. In these organizations there is always a lot said about the need for new and creative ideas. However, if those in charge like order and are uncomfortable with change, the creative people may be stopped from functioning in an optimal way.

You may have lost interest in your work if the job that you were excited about has turned into a job that no longer fits your Preference Profile. You may still like your career, but not your job. Is anyone in your career field doing a job that you would like to have? Again, don't worry yet about whether it is practical to make a change; just consider what you would really like to do with your working life.

Then you need to consider the specific benefits and the hazards of making a change.

What are the benefits of making a change?

One very good reason for changing is to keep our sanity, and another is to keep our health. Staying where we are may not drive us crazy or ruin our health, but we may be so unhappy that we are impossible to live with, so our marriage may go on the rocks.

Perhaps the best reason of all for a change is to make our lives much more enjoyable. As they say, "We only go around once, we might as well enjoy it."

Money may be a good reason for a change, although again it may be a good reason to stay. Maybe we want to live in another part of the country, and that is why we want to change.

Sometimes we get into a rut and even though we are very good at what we do, we begin to have doubts about our abilities in areas where we may have let our expertise become outdated. It may be worth a change just to refresh our abilities in a field of expertise that we like. Scientists who are promoted to managerial positions often return to research after a few years because they want to keep in touch with the latest developments in their fields.

Why should you change your job or career? You should consider all of the reasons for changing before you worry about the negative sides of any of these reasons. Like me, you may find it helpful to make a list of all the reasons for changing your employment. I wanted a new job because it would give me:

1. a new boss
2. less job pressure
3. the chance to regain self-respect in my work and as a person
4. new challenges
5. everyday tasks I would enjoy
6. more freedom of action
7. new things to learn

What are the costs of making a change?

There are costs to almost everything that we do. The best things in life are not necessarily free. Anything that takes something out of us needs to be considered a cost. The cost is in money, time, position, stress, unhappiness, energy, or even health.

It is important at this point not to say, "I don't care about the cost." If you move it will affect your children, and your spouse may have to leave his or her job. Consider what this will do to them, how they will feel.

Before you make a decision, you may want to make a list covering all its foreseeable costs to you and your family. Your family should be involved in this important exercise. If your main reason for wanting a change is a larger salary so that you can buy more for your spouse and kids, ask them about it. I have six kids and they would often complain that we did not have enough money. I would tell them that I could make more money but I would be away on business trips most of the time. They always said they wanted me home. It was nice to hear that they loved me more than money.

As you list all of the costs of the change, consider the needs and wants of your loved ones. It has been said that many a rich person forgot those who loved them as they went up the organizational ladder. In the end they ended up with their money and the friends that their money could rent.

After you have listed the costs of a proposed change in your career or in your job, it is time to consider the risks.

What are the risks of making a change?

There are a number of risks involved in making a change, any change. Things may not always come out the way we planned. I have a friend who quit her job and planned to go back to school to advance herself. A few months later she became very ill and was hospitalized for a long time. She later decided not to go back to school and now has a good job with the organization where she had been working.

Another friend took a new job complete with a big raise; the job sounded as if it was just what he wanted. I am not sure what happened, but within three months he was on the street looking for a new job. Something did not come out the way it was planned. If he had taken a good look at the real requirements of the new job, at his new boss, and at his Preference Profile, he might have refused the job when it was offered.

Listing all the things that could go wrong, and studying that list, will help you minimize the risks when you make your change. Every time we drive our car we risk being in a road accident, but we take that risk because of the benefits gained from personal transportation. However, it is not necessary to take an extra risk by not wearing seat belts, yet about 80 percent of drivers don't.

You don't need to know the exact odds of each risk— just high or low is close enough. If you have a bad accident in a car and you don't have your seat belt on, the odds are very high that you will be seriously hurt. With your seat belt on, the odds of a serious injury are low. If you take a new job that doesn't work out and you end up looking for a job in ninety days, can you and your family survive financially? Financial survival is something that can be planned for. Like auto accidents, job placements accidents do occur. Your new job may not work out the way you planned.

After you and your family have considered the benefits, the costs, and the risks, it is time to look at the practical side of a change.

Should you hang in there?

"Should I hang in there or make a change?" is a question that by itself can cause a great deal of adverse stress. In many cases we may be in the position of being damned if we do and damned if we don't. Even though the grass looks greener over the fence, we know that out there, there are thistles to stick us, rocks to trip us, and potholes for us to fall into.

I am assuming that at this point you do have some choices: you haven't been fired, there are no layoffs scheduled that will affect you, and the boss hasn't shown any obvious signs of de-hiring you. You are just seriously looking for ways to get more satisfaction out of your work.

It is very important to consider a move with due deliberation. If you're feeling a lot of pressure, it is very easy to ignore some vital facts or feelings. It is also very hard to be rational when you are depressed. You can get help from your spouse, from close and trusted friends, from counselors, from anyone who can be honest as a sounding board. The aim is to make sure you do not overlook some vital information as you make this crucial decision. But finally, you must decide whether to hang in there or move.

Making the tough personal decisions

Many of us have spent a good portion of our working lives making decisions. However, most of these decisions involve spending other people's money—our employer's. But a decision to change job or career will not only involve our own money but also may directly affect what we do for the rest of our lives.

As far as the actual work is concerned, we must consider what we like to do, what we can do, and what we can learn to do. We must also consider the overall effects of the decision, and the problems of recovering from the decision if we want to reverse it.

We must consider the timing—when different things will be happening that could result in success or failure from the decision. We must also consider new physical things inherent in the decision, such as the need for a new home, office, car, or even a new computer. Finally, and most important, are the people involved in, or affected by, the decision.

In making the decision to move, the people considerations may far outweigh the job considerations. We have all known people who have lived in one part of the country all of their lives. They know the area and all of their relatives are there. But when the kids are grown, they move across the country. Now there are weddings "back home" and grandchildren born back home, and before long they move back home where they belong.

In making any decision it is possible to choose between only two alternatives at one time. In this case, we are choosing between our current position and a potential new position. If the new position is a real job offer, we must work a little faster to make the decision to go or stay. If we don't make the decision, we are, in fact, making it by default, and so we stay where we are.

In order to compare two things and to choose between them, it is important to look at the same data. Using the Preference Profile again can help you do that.

How to compare possible job choices

You have drawn your personal Preference Profile by charting your ranking of people, things, order, and change. You have also noted those activities that you like to do, those activities that you can do well, and those that you can learn to do. You have described your current job and your ideal job in terms of the Preference Profile. Now do the same for the new employment you are seriously thinking about. You are looking for any overriding factors that can influence your decision.

One very serious question for me was the moving of my family. My wife is a teacher and it would be difficult for her to find another job without a serious financial loss. Furthermore, we live within a few hours' drive of San Francisco, a city we love to visit. Four of our six children are enrolled in local schools, and to move would disrupt their education and friendships.

We decided against digging up these roots. In contrast, some friends of ours decided to move permanently. It turned out in the end to be the right decision but they had a few little surprises. They shipped most of their belongings and then drove across the country with the kids, the dog, and all the little things that the movers didn't take. The car was stuffed full and the only safe place for the wife's prize young geranium was on her lap. After they arrived in Southern California and found geraniums growing wild she just abandoned it in a trash can.

Little surprises we can all take in stride, but the big ones can create a great deal of tension. I've heard of people who have accepted a new job, quit their old job, moved across the country into their new house, and reported for work only to be told that the organization had just started a reduction in staff. They were given one month's salary in lieu of notice.

In our case, there were serious financial factors—such as seniority, retirement, and fringe benefits—that we had to consider when I was thinking of moving to new employment. But like many other people, I had to balance these financial benefits against the job pressure. Sometimes as the pressure increases, our options seem to decrease as we lose our emotional and physical health. One difficult compromise that some people accept is to work in another city and come home only for the weekends.

There are unknowns and risks in any decision, but they will be minimized if you gather all the data you can in the time you have. Then you must make a decision that balances feelings and logic. Neither should dominate. You must balance food for the belly with food for the heart. I have known people who have turned down jobs for good and logical reasons even though they were out of work. They waited and found a job that was much more to their liking, that had a much better fit with their own Preference Profiles. Of course, there are others who have waited and then were disappointed.

When the time comes for a job change you will have to make the big leap. You can't jump a chasm in two little jumps. Start practicing ahead of time for the big leap.

Getting yourself ready for a new job and a new beginning

As soon as you decide you may need a new job, you should start looking. The longer you wait, the more stress may build up inside you. Then you may get into a panic about finding *any* new job, just as long as it is a change. The more panic you feel, the less able you are to do the proper preparation for the job search or to have good interviews. An interview is difficult at best; if panic sits beside you and you don't get the job, you will have a greater feeling of depression. While you are waiting out the time on the old job, feeling unwanted can have a very negative effect on your self-image.

You need to feel wanted

Sometimes our social life is the best place to keep alive the feelings that someone cares. In the right social group, we can feel that we are liked for who we are as a person and not for how much money or power we have. Although there are some groups that are very restrictive as to whom they will accept as members, there are many other groups where we can feel at home.

I have belonged to groups devoted to some physical activities such as climbing mountains, running rivers, and dancing; and I have even spent some time in a rodeo arena. I have belonged to groups that were involved in less strenuous activities such as photography, eating gourmet food, or studying interesting books. I have also belonged to labor unions and professional organizations. On the spiritual side, I have been involved in a number of different religious activities.

All of these different groups and activities helped me to feel better about myself and to grow as a person. Each group helped me in a different way, and I have changed groups as my needs changed. I am now involved in some new groups, I have dropped others, and I am still active in a few after many years. I have also become active again in some groups that I had dropped.

One way you can get started with a group is to talk to your friends about where they go and what they do. You need to start with friends you feel good about being with. You need to tell them what you are looking for in a group or activity. After you have been with the group for awhile, you need to get actively involved.

No matter how we are doing at work or how badly we feel about getting along in life, we all need to have someplace where we can feel okay about ourselves. We all need a way to get our emotional batteries charged, to be able to face Monday morning with renewed faith in ourselves and renewed faith that all is not bleak.

Renewing your old skills

One of the facts of life is that as we get older, we forget a lot of things that we learned when we were young. Of course, we learn a lot of new things along the way, but sometimes the new things may not seem very important. What has happened to many of us is that when we lost faith in ourselves, we forgot how much we knew; we only remember how much we've forgotten. This is amplified when younger people are hired and they have "all the right answers." At least when we are down, we think it seems that way to the boss.

When we are feeling good about ourselves, we can see which parts of what the new employee is saying are not really new but are new jargon for the same things that we were saying when we were brash new employees with all the answers. It has been said that if we understand the subject, we can explain it in simple words. But alas, when we put new jargon into simple words, we can become very unpopular with new staff members because it takes some of the mystique out of their area of specialty.

What are your real skills? It is important to take a good skills inventory of all of the things that you can do. You may have skills that you have not used for a long time, especially if you have become very highly specialized within your career field. One way to recheck your skills is to look at what other people in your career field are doing. You should ask yourself the question, "Could I do that?". If you say "Yes" or even "I think so," then you can list that activity as a viable skill. As you do this, a wonderful thing can happen: by seeing your skills in a new light, you renew your faith in your ability. If listing your skills does nothing more than renew your faith in yourself, then that alone makes it worth the effort. You then need to check those skills that need to be renewed or updated, and list ways that you can renew them.

Making sure you develop skills you like

A new job may require skills that you have never had time to develop. This is even truer if you change careers. To develop new skills, you should look very closely at the things that successful people in the field are doing and make sure that what they do is what you want to do. To make sure that this is the career area you really want, you need to recheck both your current skills and your new, needed skills and compare them with your Preference Profile. If you really don't get satisfaction out of doing what they are doing, you may not be any better off in their kind of work than you are in your current work. A good close look at all of the activities associated with a potential new job may convince you that you definitely do or do not want to spend the next few years in that type of work.

I remember when I was facing a possible layoff and I was considering some career options. Since I was raised on a mountain ranch and had some wonderful memories, my wife and I talked about the possibility of moving to a ranch. We read the real estate ads and looked at a number of properties. Then I took a good look at ranching from an adult point of view. To manage a productive working ranch, the rancher has to like order, not only in the bookkeeping but in equipment maintenance and many other important activities. A successful rancher's need to be around people would be low and an interest in change would be useful mainly to assure the order of things.

I dislike bookkeeping, and I have a low priority for neatness. I like to think about change, and I like to be around people. Though I like to work with things, I do not like to do maintenance work. I do not have the basic characteristics to be a good, productive, and happy rancher. A close look at the real job of ranching convinced me, much to my wife's relief, that I did not want to be a rancher.

Before you spend a lot of effort to develop new skills, you should make sure they are the skills that you want to use.

Knowing your skills

After you have refreshed your old skills and planned ways to develop some new ones, you need to write a condensation of your skills so that you can talk about what you can do. Making a general outline listing the major skills and the specific skills of each general area is easy to do. This outline needs to be brief so that you can use it to write resumes and expand on it for different interviews. You will need to be able to talk with confidence and honesty about all of your skills both old and new.

Finding your new job

When you reach a point where you decide you should make a move—then what? How do you look for a job, and what kind of job do you look for?

If I were to consider changing jobs again, I would find it helpful to summarize in clear and personal terms what I want and what I would not accept. In my case, one item might be, "I will not move for the next four years, but I will commute into the city." I would compare the problems of my current job with the problems of being unemployed and looking for a job. That would help me look at both the practical and the emotional side of the decision to quit.

It is also important for us to do the best we can for our current employer while we are hunting for a new job. The better the references we can get, the better off we will be. And if we don't do good work, we may well be out the door before we had planned on leaving. I would also consider how to make my

current job more tolerable while I hunted for a new job.
Here it is important to consider how the boss is treating me
and what he seems to think about my work.

After you take a close look at your current job, you need
to consider exactly why you feel down about it and discuss
those feelings with your spouse, friends, and possibly your
children.

Using career counselors

The term "career counselor" is a general term that covers
vocational counseling, personal assistance counseling, life
work planning counseling, rehabilitation counseling, and other
areas.

What can these people do for us? They will *not* find us a
job. They will *not* tell us what we want to do. In short, they
cannot live our life for us. It is our life and we must make the
decisions about how we want to live it.

A word of caution: There are some people who think they
can make your life decisions better than you can. I know an
elderly lady who lived in the same apartment for many years.
After retirement she moved to a smaller but new apartment.
She hired an interior decorator from a large department store
to help her pick out a few new things. He told her that all the
furnishings she had and loved were old and should be given
away. He then sold her all new furnishings, including a large
painting. She didn't like the painting or the furniture, but the
interior decorator told her that she should have it because it
all looked so nice together. She still does not like the painting
or the furniture, but she keeps them because "an expert" told
her that's what she should have.

I know that when I am under a lot of stress I sometimes
find it hard not to listen to, and blindly follow, the advice
given by "the experts." I think this is because we all tend to
lose faith in our own abilities when we are being adversely
affected by stress.

Another important caution: all career counselors were
not created equal, nor can they all give (sell) us the same type
of service. We must know what kind of help we need and

where to find it. A good way to start might be to make a list
of all the career counseling services in your locale, then
contact them systematically and find out what you'll be
getting for your money. Florence Lewis has done that for the
San Francisco Bay Area in her book, *Help Wanted: A Guide
to Career Counseling in the Bay Area*.* There may be
services that you could use but never knew were available.
Most people in any service industry will expand their services
to meet the needs of any paying client. Find out what the
counseling offices offer before you tell them what you need.
Then tell them what services you want only after you have
completed your own list of all the services available and their
cost. You may need the services of several organizations.
Some organizations are basically career counselors specializing
in helping you find out what you want to do. Others,
described later, are really placement agencies specializing in
helping you find a job once you know what you want.

The search for a new job

Once you know what kind of work you want, finding a job is
the next step. There are basically four ways to find a job:
word of mouth, job ads, job placement services, and
pounding the pavement.

   Word of mouth means knowing someone who knows
someone. There's nothing wrong with finding out about a job
through a friend. You should consider who you know that
may have an "in" in any appropriate organization.

   I know of a number of jobs that were created because an
organization found out that a specific individual was looking
for a new job. Someone in the organization knew the
individual either in person or by reputation, and wanted to
use his or her very specialized talents. The job that was
created was not charity: the organization had a specific need
but did not feel it could find one individual who could fill the
vacancy.

Oakland, CA: Two Step Books, 1978.

Of course, there is a level of luck in being in the right place at the right time. Many jobs, particularly at the higher levels within an organization, are filled through knowing the right people even though the job may appear in a positions available ad. The individual may have already been selected for that position and the posting of the job was a mere formality.

Job ads are published in newspapers, journals, and the lists put out by unions and professional societies. You need to read them all. Many entry-level jobs are listed in the help wanted section of the newspaper and mid-level professional jobs are listed in journals. High-level jobs sometimes are not advertised at all, although this is rarer these days because of various government and industry policies to expand opportunities in employment. If an organization advertises for a specific type of personnel and you have a background in a different area, you should not despair. The organization may be going through a growth period and will need people in several specialties.

Placement services are available through public agencies, labor and professional organizations, and commercial enterprises. The public services, and labor and professional organizations will generally give you only a listing of specific positions that are available. It is up to you to obtain the new job listings and then to follow up.

Some commercial job placement enterprises charge for placing you in a job and others charge only the employer. The former require you to pay either in advance or after they have helped you find a job. You need to make sure that you know what you are paying for. Some agencies have a small service fee (about $25) to discourage those who are only casually interested in their services. However, you need to make sure that your service fee will get you more than a copy of the help wanted ads from the local newspaper.

Executive search firms seem to take one of two approaches. They will either send your resume to every organization that is looking for someone with roughly your qualifications, or they will select the resumes of only three or four people and submit these to the employer. Executive search firms who make a careful selection take great pride in always placing one of the three or four candidates they introduce.

From my experience, the placement organizations that send out resumes to many firms seem to want resumes submitted in their standard formats, perhaps to allow cross-checking by a computer. They seem more interested in the resume than in what an individual really likes or wants to do.

The other type of search organization does an in-depth study of open positions and then searches out the people who may fit into the positions. The agency often contacts people who are not even looking for a new job but whom it feels would be right for a particular position. The search firm then interviews the possible candidates at length and recommends three or four to the organization with the opening.

There are now many placement firms specializing in specific career areas or levels of expertise.

Pounding the pavement means going to various companies who are hiring and asking about the jobs that they have available. Many large organizations have a new listing of open jobs each week, so you need to keep checking. It will save traveling time to make a list of the places that you intend to go to and fit them into an itinerary. It also helps to keep track of the places that you have been and the names of everyone you talked to. Calling the receptionist by name (the correct name) may be to your advantage when you come back for an interview.

If I were looking for a job, I would make several lists: all of the friends who may know of a job or be of help in the search; all of the publications that carry help wanted or positions available ads; all the job placement agencies that may be of help; and all of the trade and professional organizations that provide listings.

Resumes and interviews

There are several good books available on developing and writing resumes; some are noted in the extract from Florence Lewis's *Help Wanted: A Guide to Career Counseling in the Bay Area* that is included at the end of this book. Career counselors, some placement agencies, or a professional writer may be able to help you prepare resumes that reflect both you and the types of organizations you want to work for. There is no one format for a resume that is right for all circumstances.

I remember how difficult it was for me to write a resume. After I had been with the same organization for a number of years and because my self-image had deteriorated to a very low level, I had difficulty identifying any skills and abilities that would be of any use to anyone. The only way I could get started was to make a list of everything I had ever done. I included some things that I did not do well along with those I did do well. I then divided these activities into categories, including some activities in several different categories. This exercise helped me to focus on some of the more positive aspects of my life, and that was a reward in itself.

From such notes and lists you can tailor a resume to fit each prospective job opening.

A job interview can be a dreadful or an exciting experience. How you feel will depend on you and the interviewer. Since you can't do much about the interviewer, you must concentrate on the interviewee: that's you.

With a good self-image, you may feel scared at interviews but will find them exciting. You know you are good and your confidence will show. But if you haven't worked on your self-image, you will feel both scared and depressed. Deep inside you will feel that you can't do this job and that this feeling shows. Then when the rejection letter comes, you say to yourself, "I didn't really expect to get the job anyway." As time and more interviews pass, you get a little miffed when someone lightly suggests that you could write a book on how to write rejection letters because you have such a large collection of them.

H. Anthony Medley's book, *Sweaty Palms: The Neglected Art of Being Interviewed,** is also included in our bibliography. He covers what we need to do to get ready for an interview, some "do's" and "don'ts" about the interview, and how to be prepared for different types of interviews. He

---

Belmont, CA: Lifetime Learning Publications, 1978.

also covers the importance of enthusiasm and how to answer different types of questions.

It takes time to get experience at being interviewed, so you should interview for all the jobs you can even if you don't think you would accept some of them. If you interview for a job that you could do but might not accept if it were offered, you can relax and learn how to be interviewed. It will give you a chance to practice some of the things covered in *Sweaty Palms*. There may be a second bonus: you may be told that you are overqualified for the job. When you are rebuilding your self-respect, few things sound better than, "I wish we could afford you for we would like you to join our staff." Perhaps the only greater reassurance is, "We are offering you the position." Even when you are among the top few candidates for a job and don't get it, it feels good to know that there are some who think very highly of your ability.

Feeling a personal growth

When we talk to others about our skills and our abilities and they have positive responses, we begin to feel more positive about ourselves. This is a very important part of our personal growth. The nice thing about this type of growth cycle is that the more positive things we hear about ourselves, the more positive we feel about ourselves and the more positive we sound about ourselves, and so things start getting better and better.

As you hear good things about yourself, write them down. As you reread them, it will make you feel better about yourself. Be honest and write exactly what was said or as close as you can remember it.

Hearing positive things about ourselves plants the seeds of new hope that can grow and bloom. I remember how my hope started to grow when I found that there were people in other organizations who respected and liked me—even though the feeling is not a good enough reason to accept a new job. I was experiencing that when I wrote, "Where Is It?"

Where Is It?

I wish I could see
that place in life
where there's a niche for me.

A place that feels just right
one where I can feel at ease.

A place full of love
and caring.

A place for me
where I belong.

I now know that limits on opportunity exist mainly in the mind. Although I cannot choose the path that I am to follow, I can choose my destination.

I found it helped me to make a list of all the places where people respected me, even those that could not be my employer—labor or professional societies, service clubs, social organizations, and so on. I also tried to write down the names of the people I knew in these organizations because I may have needed them as references. In some cases they knew I was looking and they put in a good word with their own employers. Your most enthusiastic job offers may well come from some organization that you haven't applied to but has heard about you from someone respected. When you are asked if you will come for an unsolicited job interview—that really feels great.

You need to keep on looking

You need to keep your list growing and make sure that you get the correct spelling for the names of both the organizations and the people. Then some fine day a real offer for a job that you really want will come in the mail. Now that's a day to remember. But there are many good reasons for not being offered a job. You may have come in second because someone else has a balance of skills that more closely

matched the job. Last-minute budget cuts may keep a job
from being filled. In that case, not being offered a job is
certainly better than being hired and then having you and the
job cut. Finding any job may take months, and finding a
specific job may take even longer.

Before the job offer finally arrives, you can keep on
building your self-confidence. At some point you'll really
know you will be getting a job offer. When I was at this
point, I wrote "The Geese and I." A short time later, when I
was leaving my old employment, I gave the group I was
working with a copy of this poem and "Safe Anchorage," the
last poem in this book.

The Geese and I

As long shadows
come in early evening,

And the nip
of first frost
fills the air,

I see the giant vees
of honking geese
flying in the setting sun.

And I, like the geese,
must go with the changing times.

But for those who stay
the snowbirds
will fill the air
around the feeders.

And for the geese and I
it is new places and new faces.

But both the geese and I
shall pass this way again.

Leaving in style

When you reach the point where you can feel good about yourself and most of the people you'll be leaving, then you may want to do some more writing. I made a mental list of the people I would miss and noted some of the good things about each.

I think one of the big steps in real personal growth is to be able to see the world from the other person's point of view. I know I, like many of my friends who have been hurt or experienced bitterness, feel their growth came when they were able to forgive. I know some who have never forgiven, and I think they are the losers. I really believe that there are very few people in the world who are really out to get someone else. Each of us is just trying to do our own job and that sometimes brings us to an impasse with someone else.

So now you're on your way. You may or may not have a going-away party but no matter how bitter you are, you should not tell the boss or your co-workers you are leaving how much you hated the place. Don't burn your bridges. It is important to leave a good last impression because someday you may be back in touch with your old employer.

Go out with your head held high. It will help you feel better about yourself.

Reevaluating your new job

One of the very important and very nice things that happens on a new job is that your new boss and your new co-workers show you that they respect and like you. Your new boss takes you around and introduces you to all the people, and says with pride, "This is our newest employee to join our group," and that feels good.

Even though there may be a hundred or more people in your new department, if you spend a little time each day learning names, before very long you will know them all.

The process of learning people's names also helps you to become one of the team and very soon you, too, will be just "one of the gang." Of course, getting along with your boss is very important. As your new boss introduces you, it will help to make a note of how you're introduced. Try to note some of your skills that the boss highlights, because they are likely to be of most benefit to the group.

Giving it your all

You have a new job and you have met many of your new co-workers. Now it is time to go to work. You and your boss think you can do the job and do it well. So you need to concentrate on that.

I know I still have some bad habits left over from old jobs, habits born from a "to hell with it" feeling about my work. Some of your old habits can keep you from doing your best on your new job. You may find at times that you are not doing your best. If so, stop right then and think about what you're feeling. Are you fearing criticism or feeling that you are no good? Are you feeling really bored with certain parts of your work? When you get a new job, it will take time to flush these old feelings out of your system. But before you can flush them out, you must first recognize them and acknowledge that they are feelings that can affect you. You need to think about those old feelings whenever they seem to be haunting you.

Developing your self-confidence

There is a vast difference between people who have self-confidence and those who don't. They look different, they act, speak, and even walk differently. The confident ones do it with style; they have a touch of class. We can't buy class but we can have it, and it is free. Class is the outward appearance of an inward feeling of self-confidence. That doesn't mean we have to "know it all"; in fact, on the contrary, we know that we don't know it all, but we are not ashamed of not knowing. We are not ashamed of being wrong, and we learn from every experience.

I think there are times when we all feel like a whimpering puppy dog with its tail between its legs. That is not class.

To learn to do it with style, we must first get to know ourselves better. There are times when we all feel ill at ease, but when we are ill at ease, we may not be doing it with style.

I remember speaking to the local school board. Even though I had strong feelings about the subject, I was ill at ease. I didn't feel very confident in myself. After I sat down I had even less confidence, and others later confirmed that I didn't give a good presentation. I did not do it with style. At that time I was at a low ebb of self-confidence. I have now developed a much higher level of self-confidence, and I have also made a number of presentations that I felt were given with style.

To develop self-confidence we must recognize the situations where we don't have it. I found it helpful to make a mental list of situations in which I am likely to feel a lack of confidence, fear of criticism, or uncertainty about what is right. After I recall my ill-at-ease feelings, I try to find a pattern of specific conditions that bring on the feelings, then I try to find the cause and correct it.

In time I have been able to broaden the area where I feel at ease and can do more things "with style."

The new job's Preference Profile

After you've been on your new job long enough to get a feeling for what it's all about, you may find that the work is not exactly what you had expected it to be. When this happens, it is time to do a new job Preference Profile to identify what your new work is really like. Then check to make sure that your personal Preference Profile and your new job's Preference Profile still match.

Ask yourself if this is the work you really want to do and how it will go in the next few years. No matter how good a match you and your job have, there'll always be some aspects about it that you will not like, some things you have to do that you will not find exciting. During the early months in the job, you have to give these tasks as much care and attention as you do the tasks that you like. Otherwise, the boss may see an uneven job performance and feel uncertain about which tasks you can do well. We are no different from our bosses in this way: once we become uncertain about what someone else will do, we become reluctant to assign them tasks in which we have a large stake in the outcome. Most of us have had subordinates or co-workers whom we just would not trust with important tasks.

If the boss cannot trust us with important tasks, our chances for promotion may well be slim and our job longevity short. To make sure we don't do an uneven job, we need to identify all of the tasks we don't like to do, then concentrate on doing them well.

Your "don't like" list should add up to only a small part of your working time. If you find you have to spend too much of your time doing things you don't like to do, then maybe you have picked the wrong job. Or maybe, as you get into your new work, you can reshape your job so that you spend more time on tasks that fit your preferences.

The new boss's Preference Profile

After you have become comfortable with your new job, it may be helpful to go over your Preference Profile with your boss. Then you might ask your boss to fill out his or her own Preference Profile, compare it with your own, and use the comparison as a starting point to discuss the areas that you both appear to find interesting and the areas where you won't have much common interest. If you have a boss that will do this, you can probably also discuss the best way to deal with the areas where you do not have a common interest.

You need to be specific about how you can assure yourself that your new boss will do things WITH you and not TO you, FOR you, or WITHOUT you. A discussion of personal and job preferences can help you and your boss to communicate *with* each other.

When you know you belong

When we first join an organization, we are generally given the "red carpet treatment." We should enjoy it while it lasts, because it won't last long. Our boss has many things to think about, and soon we'll be just one of the staff. The sooner the label of "new employee" wears off, the sooner we can begin to feel that we really belong. The sooner we feel we really belong, the sooner we can forget about watching the help wanted ads.

On a new job I have sometimes felt that "they" didn't like me anymore, and then sometimes that I belonged. These feelings can affect how we behave. There may be an initial period of unbelieving, of wondering if it's really real, a time when we are not at all sure that it will all work out. Of course, keeping it real and keeping our job are things we should work at daily. Happiness is something we find daily along the way and not at the end of the road.

It is important for you to learn to know your feelings, your new boss, and your new job. Then the time comes for you to find out more about how you have changed.

Your rebirth as a person

After you have been on a new job for a while, you may be pleasantly surprised to find a new person in the mirror each morning. You may be smiling a lot more, and those deep frown lines may have gone from your face. You may laugh a lot more, and your friends and loved ones may confirm that you are a lot easier to live with.

Before you forget about them, go back and think about some of the things that have happened recently which helped build your feelings of pride in yourself.

A job well done and you feel great

You have grown in your ability to do your new job, and you should also be renewing old skills and learning some new ones. There will be ups and downs, but by remembering your up feelings about

121

specific tasks well done, you can reinstate your feelings of worthwhileness.

Some of our co-workers on a new job become friends. Even though we may not see them except at work, they are an important part of our lives. It is these close work-related friends who can help keep us on the positive personal growth path, and we can help them do the same. It is these trusted friends who can say to us, "You really blew it at the staff meeting today" or say, "Wow! That was a great presentation." In both of these cases we know they are honest and telling us what they really believe. A good friend is one of the world's most precious treasures but like many treasures, friendship is fragile and must be cared for. It cannot be all giving or all receiving.

I remember a friend from work with whom I shared many close feelings. At one time he became very down and needed more and more of my time just in listening to him let off steam. He, however, never had time to listen to me. He needed more than I could give and as a result I drifted away. I can also remember some of my friends who drifted away when I was down because I was not listening to their feelings.

When we are sharing we are growing and we can enjoy each other's company, but when we are not sharing we may stop growing and lose interest in the relationship. Each person is the loser.

Your old boss through new eyes

It has been said in many lands and in many tongues, "Hatred destroys the hater, not the hated." If you have left your old job under less than desirable circumstances, you may well have some strong negative feelings about your old boss. It is important that you get rid of these feelings.

Keeping a strong, vindictive feeling can do more harm to you than it can to your old boss. After all, at this stage you are most interested in you and your own personal growth. You shouldn't let harbored ill-feelings keep you from growing.

I know I have felt and some of my friends have felt

periods of great personal growth. We have a great new feeling of openness. I was feeling that way when I wrote "Spring Flower."

Spring Flower

Like a crocus
set out
in a little clay pot

My roots grew
cramped but strong.

And now
like the crocus
whose pot
has been cast aside

My roots grow deep
in the moist soil.

And in the warm spring sun
I too will come to full bloom.

When I wrote this, I reaffirmed that only in a world of trust and love can we unfold and bloom. And on a good job, you can feel the worth of caring and the opportunities to grow as a person. You have a chance to "show your stuff," to demonstrate your skills—and also to grow as a person. Our personal growth is enhanced when we approach life with malice toward none and charity toward all.

Your new sense of worth

Growing as a person is not based on learning any specific skills. It is a matter of getting to know *ourselves* better—not only our own skills but also our ability to respond to new situations, to feel more comfortable with ourselves, and more self-assured.

My growth has always seemed to be in quantum steps. Some of these steps have been painful and some pleasant, but all exciting to look back on. I once wrote that I had grown a great deal in the previous years and could not see how much more I could grow as a person. But now I can look back to where I was then and see how far I have come.

At one time I was growing more self-confident as a speaker, but not as a writer. Now I am comfortable as a speaker and am gaining confidence as a writer. At one time I did not show my feelings but now I am much more comfortable showing them. My oldest daughter says she can remember me as being stoic, yet now I am quick to smile. I can remember when I didn't know what the expression "growing as a person" really meant. Now I think I do.

It is important to remember what we have done in life and how we know we have grown as a person. By remembering, you learn more about you. It has been said that the farther back you can look, the farther forward you may be able to see.

I have found as I've gotten older, I feel I am of more worth, not in material things but as a person. I feel of more worth to myself, my loved ones, and to all of humanity. I think it is interesting that some of the young look at forty as over the hill, and many of us who are well over forty look back and can say how young and naive we were then. I can only hope I never "grow up" if growing up means to stop growing. High school class reunions are sometimes interesting because so many who seemed grown up when they graduated from high school have, alas, grown since then in girth but not as persons. They seem of no more worth to themselves or to society now than they were then.

We need to consider our worth as a person, not by how much money we make or how many people we control. It is really not how much we have but how much we enjoy life that makes for happiness.

To me, worth is measured by how much we give of ourselves for the betterment of others. It has been said that "Politicians worry about the next election, and statesmen worry about the next generation." I feel the statesman is of more worth than the politician. But that is my definition of worth. You must measure your worth by your own definition.

New directions

With a clearer sense of my current worth, I can see the directions I want to go to be of even greater worth. These new directions are often at complete odds with where I thought I was headed just a few years ago. It was not long ago that I needed to hear the praise of others and I did many things to enlist their approval. I am not saying that I no longer like and need praise, but I now do more to please me. I like to be satisfied personally with what I have done at the end of each day.

More than before, I now like to help people grow in their ability to do what they like to do. I also like to find new uses for things and to understand the links between things and people. I now find that my writing helps me to understand how people feel and what we all can do to help ourselves grow. Though I am learning more about the technical side of photography my strongest interest is what people feel when they see my photographs. I am proudest of the photographs that have captured one of those fleeting moments of serenity in the lives of man and nature. These are the types of activities I most enjoy. Now I just need to figure out how to make a living doing them.

The bitter and the sweet

With every job there is the good and the bad, and like many others, I have had a few jobs that were more bad than good. Since I am now in a good cycle and things are getting better, I can look back and see the rocks and pitfalls that nearly did me in. But I rubbed my bruises and went on. Early one January I wrote "Old Calendar."

Old Calendar

*As I took the old calendar
from the wall*

*I mused, it's been a good year
all in all.*

It had been a rough year, but it had been a good year: I had grown. Most of all I had gained a new sense of direction for my life and a new appreciation for my work.

Your life beyond the job

For most of us, our job takes up a lot of our time, forty to sixty hours or more per week. Many of us tend to let our lives revolve around our work. But there is more to life than our work, our boss's needs, and our needs for money. We can expand our interests. We can stop working through our lunch hour, stop taking work home. We can find some time to call our own.

It has been said that if you want something done, ask a busy person. Many of us take on almost every task that is offered at work or in the community. We continuously feel rushed and have no time to relax, no time for our families.

I learned to say NO and have found that all the activities I have said no to get done by somebody else. Now before I take on a new activity I do a mental job Preference Profile, then I ask myself why I should be doing the activity. Some jobs really do not need to be done now while others do, particularly when the boss says, "I want it now." In my outside activities, of course, I have more choice and I have found that I am now happier doing fewer things than I did before. I do them better and feel better about them. With my four sons I have been involved with Boy Scouts for many years. I was the Scout troop committee treasurer for a while and this meant doing just the thing I dislike most. But like many of us, I said yes in a weak moment. After a while I finally said no, and a man who is an accountant took over the job. It was a natural for him and he very much enjoyed helping the troop in this way. I have also enjoyed my work with the Girl Scouts and Campfire Girls, and doing things with my two daughters.

I feel that my outside activities have helped me keep a better self-image during those periods when I was having some down feelings about my work.

Getting involved with activities beyond and separate from work can give a new sense of value of yourself and your accomplishments. Consider some of the things that you are doing in your non-work world. Should you stop doing some things that you do not enjoy? Consider how much you are in control of your life and how much other people are running your life for you. Each time you take back part of your life and run it for yourself, you grow as a person.

Knowing you are on the way up

The often-heard refrain "TGIF" or "Thank God It's Friday" heralds the weekend and implies enjoyment. Ah, the weekend—a chance to *mow* the lawn, *trim* the hedge, and maybe even *drive* to the dump. For this we say TGIF? Yes, because we are doing things more or less of our own choosing.

Life is more enjoyable when we feel good about what we are doing and who we are doing it with. A trip to the dump generally does not rate as a high point in our lives. Yet we do it, and feel good about how much better the yard or the attic looks. Feeling a sense of pride in *everything* we do increases our enjoyment of our work and our lives as a whole. As each day comes, we can unwrap it as a precious gift which we can then take time to cherish.

I have told my kids that when I was in school I shoveled our dairy barns. I was proud of how clean they looked when I finished the job. We can find something to be proud of in any honorable work, some way to have pride about ourselves.

Pride in work also increases the quality of the work output. Pride in workmanship, whether wood carving or computer programming, can be contagious. Some groups in an organization seem to put out a better quality of work than other similar groups. There often seems to be a sense of levity in the good producers, but these lighthearted people often outproduce the other groups in both quantity and quality. In less productive work groups, TGIF seems to be the prevailing attitude.

If you can't remember many things with pride because you haven't been proud of your activities, maybe now is a good time to start working on your pride. Re-check your activities to see how well they fit your Preference Profile.

Loving yourself

To love our neighbors we must first love ourselves. To love ourselves we must be proud of ourselves. This does not mean pride that says, "I'm better than you" but rather pride that says, "I'm better than I used to be." When we feel good about ourselves, we can give of ourselves. There is a big difference between giving of ourselves and yielding of ourselves. We give from a point of strength and take joy in giving, but we yield from a point of weakness and may hate those who take from us.

I have been active with the Boy Scout troop not so much from a sense of obligation as simply liking most of the activities. But I can now see that I was talked into being treasurer and I said yes from a point of weakness. I did not like the job and did not feel good about doing it.

Consider how you feel about yourself at work and away from work. When you say yes, are you giving or yielding? Do others give to you or do they have to yield to you, or you to them?

In order to give and receive freely we must put down our swords and shields. But to put down our armament we must first trust others.

Learning to trust again

There is a level of trust that may represent foolhardiness. I
don't leave the keys in my car or my house unlocked because
there are strangers I don't know if I can trust or not. Our six
kids and their friends add up to a lot of people coming and
going at our house. We have many nice things—a lot of tools
and camping gear, and a large library. Friends and neighbors
have borrowed and returned almost everything but we have
lost many items over the years. I think most were misplaced
or forgotten but I am sure a few were stolen. We would have
many more items today if we had not so openly trusted
people, but we would have lost a lot more of ourselves.

I think the more we trust our co-workers and our bosses,
the more we feel good about ourselves. Can you trust them
with your best interest or do you feel that would be
foolhardy? Trusting is a process of everyone putting down
their swords and shields together and then beating them into
plowshares. After we have learned to love ourselves and to
trust others, we can then learn to love others.

Learning to share your love again

When a co-worker has been sick and we politely ask, "How
do you feel?" and we barely hear the response, that is not
love. When we care, we really hear what is said.

Love is a wonderful thing because it grows and grows
and there seems to be no limit to how far it can go. As each
of our children was born, our love for the others did not
diminish but simply grew to include each new child. There
are six of them and as they marry and have children, our love
grows even more.

Our love for family, friends, neighbors, co-workers, and
bosses can grow if we are willing to let it grow. As we become
more open about our feelings about others, they get to know
the real us a little better. The more people know the real us,
the more they will trust us and the more opportunities they
will give us when they need our trust. There are some

technical matters that I feel "stupid" not knowing, but I have friends of whom I can ask those "dumb" questions. Of course, they in turn can talk with me about their inner feelings. The growth of our trust and love is mutual.

New ventures

With a greater trust and sharing of love will come more opportunities to grow as a person. You will get new opportunities to take on new challenges, meet new people, and expand your world.

We have a group of foreign scientists visiting our laboratory for a year. Because I now feel good about myself and can judge the amount of time I can use for fun projects with them, I offered to help them with their command of the English language. They are wonderful people whom I never would have met if I had not taken on the new venture. I enjoy their company both professionally and socially.

New ventures and opportunities can add a level of exciting stress to your life. This type of stress will not adversely affect you as long as you feel good about your job, feel good about your boss, and most of all feel good about yourself.

For everyone who takes time to try new ventures, to rest, to grow, and go out again, I wrote "Safe Anchorage."

Safe Anchorage

May your anchorage
always be sheltered
from the storm.

And in the early morning mist
may you hear the fish jump
and the birds sing softly.

And may the sun fill
your heart
as it does the day
with warmth.

Though your ship may be safe in a harbor, that is not what your ship was built for. Take your ship and seek new horizons, use your harbor only for a resting place and not a final destination.

One of your never ending ventures will be improving your job, your relations with your boss, and the new you— your total new life. This venture goes on even after you can say I am happy and proud of my job, my boss, and me.

Glossary

This glossary and much of the bibliography that follows it are reprinted, with permission, from *Help Wanted: A Guide to Career Counseling in the Bay Area* by Florence Lewis, published in 1978 by Two Step Books, P.O. Box 2942, Oakland, CA 94618.

Assessment.   A blanket term referring to determining (by testing exercises, interviews, or some combination of these methods) which career or careers suit you. Assessment can be done by your counselor, by you, in a group or in some combination. Assessment should help you make a decision about what career you might want to pursue. Some topics covered in Assessment are:

> *Skills and Aptitudes*.   Generally, this means what you know how to do, and what you could do if given the training. Measurement of aptitudes, like measurement of intelligence, is influenced by many factors not controlled by the testing procedures; the traditional testing of aptitudes is currently done infrequently. Employment Development Department offices offer some testing in this vein. A few career counselors offer it.

> *Determining Skills*.   On the surface this appears to be a straightforward procedure, but it is more complicated than it looks. According to Dr. Sidney Fine, the founder of the

Dictionary of Occupational Titles, we all have three different types of skills. Everyone has some specific job-related skills, such as typing, cooking, driving, sawing. These skills are specific, rooted to certain jobs and may not necessarily be transferable from job to job. The set of skills which are functional and transferable from job to job are described in more general terms: problem solving, designing, creating, leading, organizing, etc. These skills are often what lie behind our success in, and enjoyment of our work. The third set of skills, known as self-management or adaptive skills, have to do with how we handle responsibility and how we deal with time and authority. In any career search, all of the different skills need to be taken into consideration.

Hidden Job Market.   The majority of jobs, particularly professional-level jobs, are not advertised. Most people find jobs through some form of person to person contact (through friends, in interviews) and by creating jobs. If you accept the premise of the hidden job market, then non-traditional job hunting methods must be used.

Informational Interview.   This refers to interviewing people who you identify as doing something similar to your chosen job, or someone who you think might be able to give you helpful information. This is not a job interview (although it may turn into one), but rather a way of finding out details about the work, the field, and current conditions in the market.

Interests.   The measurement of interests has long been part of vocational assessment. The Strong-Campbell Interest Inventory is a popular interest-measurement device which compares your interests to those of successful men and women in a wide variety of careers. Interest testing tends to be non-threatening because it does not deal with aptitude or ability. The Strong draws on the theories of John Holland, who divided interests into six general categories: artistic, social, enterprising, conventional, realistic and investigative. For a thorough exposition of these groups, see *Making Vocational Choices: A Theory of Careers* by John Holland.

> *Note:*   If you take the Strong, or any standardized measurement device, be sure that the person who interprets it for you knows you well enough to give the test results some depth. The Strong can be interpreted by you, if you use the instructions on the back.

Job Hunting Techniques.   This term can mean many different things. It can mean resume writing skills, interviewing skills, how to answer ads in the newspaper, how to send out broadcast letters, how to write a cover letter tailored to the job you are interested in, how to create your own job, how to dress, how to negotiate for a salary, and a myriad of other individual details involved in the job hunting process.

Job hunting techniques can also refer to an approach to looking for work which emphasizes developing contacts, doing informational interviews, and controlling the job interview.

You may need coaching in all or some of these techniques. Two of the most commonly stressed are:

Interviewing Techniques.   Interviewing for a job is a stressful situation. It is often the crucial factor in getting a job. Preparing for it, thinking about possible answers to common interviewing questions, knowing how to handle illegal and trick queries and how to be in control all can improve your chances of success.

Resume Writing.   A resume can be a work of art. Many people in the career counseling field strongly advise that you do not compose only one resume, but tailor one to meet the requirements of each job you are interested in. In addition, there are many experts who counsel many different types and creative uses of resumes. It is a good idea to read about resumes before composing yours. Expert advice can often be helpful at this phase of the career search.

Values.   This refers to what you hold to be important, what you want from a job and in your life. Power, prestige, artistic expression, home and family are examples of values. It is important to know what you value so that you can find a job which fits into your value system.

Bibliography

The books listed here are a sample of "self-help" career manuals. There are many books on related fields (such as career satisfaction, career psychology, career management), as well as specific vocations. If you are interested in pursuing these topics, ask your local librarian or a career librarian and use the various *Readers Guides to Books in Print*. Many career manuals have their own bibliographies which may give you ideas for further reading.

You can use a bibliography in a variety of ways:

Before you go to see a career counselor, you can familiarize yourself with the common terms used by career counselors. It might make it easier for you to ask questions about the process so that you will not have to cope with too much new information in the first interview.

You can try some or all of the self-directed exercises contained in many of these books to give you a better idea of where you want to go when you see a counselor.

You can use one or two of these books to help you find out exactly what you want to do and to show you the tools which you can use to get the kind of job you want.

If you are using the books as guides, you can use a counselor as a secondary resource to help you with problems the books don't cover.

137

Richard Bolles suggests that you buy a book, get two or three friends together, and tackle the career search in a group (see page 61 in *What Color is Your Parachute?*, 1978 edition).

A word about "Paper Guidance": *Paper Guidance* refers to the process of you, the career seeker, interacting with a set of paper materials designed to guide you, without help, or with only minimal help from a counselor. This means that you can go to the bookstore, buy a copy of one of the books listed below, do the exercises on your own, and go from there: all without the need for the expertise of a counselor. This concept has been pioneered by John Holland, who designed the self-administered vocational guidance tool "The Self-Directed Search," and Richard Bolles, who has written "The Quick Job Hunting Map." This paper material is designed to circumvent the need for a guide in the process of finding a career. It costs relatively little to buy a book and go through the exercises on your own. However, few of us can complete the entire process of a career search from start to finish without some contact with others who have expertise in the field and enthusiasm to offer us.

Albee, L. *Over Forty, Out Of Work*. Englewood Cliffs, New Jersey: Prentice-Hall, 1970.

Bartlett, L. E. *New Work New Life: Help Yourself To Tomorrow—A Report From People Already There*. New York: Harper & Row, 1976.

Bishop, B. *The Scratch Pad Workbook: For Creative Lifework Planning*. Berkeley, California: Ten Speed Press, 1978.

Boll, C. *Executive Jobs Unlimited*. New York: Macmillan, 1965.

Bolles, R. N. *The Quick Job Hunting Map* and *The Quick Job Hunting Map For Beginners*. Berkeley, California: Ten Speed Press, 1978.

Bolles, R. N. *The Three Boxes Of Life And How To Get Out Of Them*. Berkeley, California: Ten Speed Press, 1978.

Bolles, R. N. *What Color Is Your Parachute? A Practical Manual For Job-Hunters And Career-Changers*. Berkeley, California: Ten Speed Press, rev. 1978.

Brown, S. C. (ed.) *Changing Careers In Science And Engineering*. Cambridge: MIT Press, 1972.

Buskirk, R. H. *Your Career: How To Plan It, Manage It, Change It*. Boston: CBI Publishing, 1977.

Campbell, D. P. *If You Don't Know Where You're Going, You'll Probably End Up Somewhere Else*. Niles, Illinois: Argus, 1974.

Carkhuff, R. R., Friel, T. W., Pierce, R. M. and Willis, D. G. *Get a Job*. Amherst, Massachusetts: Human Resources Development Press, 1975.

Cosgrave, G. *Career Work Book*. Palo Alto, California: Consulting Psychologist Press, Inc., 1973.

Crystal, J. C. and Bolles, R. N. *Where Do I Go From Here With My Life?* New York: The Seabury Press, 1974.

Djeddah, E. *Moving Up: How To Get High Salaried Jobs.* Berkeley, California: Ten Speed Press, 1975.

Fensterheim, H. and Baer, J. *Don't Say Yes When You Want To Say No.* New York: Dell, 1975.

Figler, H. E. *Path: A Career Workbook for Liberal Arts Students.* Cranston, Rhode Island: The Carroll Press, 1975.

File, N. and Howroyd, B., *How To Beat The Establishment And Get That Job.* Glendale, California: Bowmar Press, 1975.

Fine, Sidney A. *Guidelines for the Design of New Careers.* Kalamazoo, Michigan: W. E. Upjohn Institute for Employment Research, 1967.

Fiore, M. V. and Strauss, P. S. *Promotable Now!* New York: John Wiley & Sons, 1972.

Flach, F. F. *Choices.* New York: Bantam Books, 1971.

Friel, T. W. and Carkhuff, R. R. *The Art of Developing A Career.* Amherst, Massachusetts: Human Development Press, 1974.

Greco, B. *How To Get The Job That's Right For You.* Homewood, Illinois: Dow Jones-Irwin, 1975.

Haldane, B. *Career Satisfaction: A Guide To Job Freedom.* New York: AMACOM, 1974.

Haldane, B. *Job Power Now: The Young People's Guide To Job Finding.* Washington, D.C.: Acropolis, 1976.

Holland, J. L. *Making Vocational Choices: A Theory Of Careers.* Englewood Cliffs, New Jersey: Prentice-Hall, 1973. (Includes "The Self-Directed Search.")

Irish, R. K. *Go Hire Yourself An Employer.* New York: Anchor Press, 1973.

Jackson, T. and Mayleas, D. *The Hidden Job Market: A System To Beat The System.* New York: Quadrangle, 1976.

Kirn, A. and Kirn, M. *Lifework Planning.* Hartford, Connecticut: Arthur G. Kirn & Associates, 1974.

Lasher, W. K. *How You Can Get A Better Job.* Chicago, Illinois: American Technical Society, 1972.

Lathrop, R. *Who's Hiring Who.* Berkeley, California: Ten Speed Press, 1977.

LeSan, E. J. *The Wonderful Crisis Of Middle Age: Some Personal Reflections.* New York: David McKay, 1973.

Lewis, Florence. *Help Wanted: A Guide To Career Counseling In The Bay Area.* Oakland, California: Two Step Books, 1978.

Loughary, J. W. and Ripley, T. M. *This Isn't Quite What I Had In Mind: A Career Planning Program For College Students.* Chicago: Follett, 1978.

Medley, H. Anthony. *Sweaty Palms: The Neglected Art Of Being Interviewed.* Belmont, California: Lifetime Learning, 1978.

Miller, A. F. and Mattson, R. T. *The Truth About You: Discover*

What You Should Be Doing With Your Life. Old Tappan, New York: Fleming H. Revell Co., 1977.

Miller, D. B. *Personal Vitality: A Life Goal, A Life And Career Strategy, A New Work Ethic, An Organization Strategy, A National Policy*. Reading, Massachusetts: Addison-Wesley, 1977.

Newman, M. and Berkowitz, B. *How To Be Your Own Best Friend*. New York: Ballantine Books, 1978.

Noer, D. *How To Beat The Employment Game*. Radnor, Pennsylvania: Chilton Book Company, 1975.

Rogers, C. R. *On Becoming A Person*. Boston: Houghton Mifflin, 1961.

Sandman, P. *The Unabashed Career Guide*. London: Collier Books, 1969.

Schoonmaker, A. M. *Executive Career Strategy*. New York: American Management Association, 1971.

Sheehy, G. *Passages*. New York: Bantam Books, 1977.

Skelton, D. *Fire Again: A Guide To Survival In The Corporate Foothills*. New York: Funk and Wagnalls, 1968.

Souerwine, A. H. *Career Strategies—Planning For Personal Achievement*. New York: AMACOM, 1978.

Splaver, S. *Non-Traditional College Routes To Careers*. New York: Messner, 1974.

Terkel, S. *Working*. New York: Avon, 1975.

Uris, A. *Thank God It's Monday*. New York: Thomas Y. Crowell, 1974.

Weiler, N. W. *Reality And Career Planning: A Guide For Personal Growth*. Reading, Massachusetts: Addison-Wesley, 1977.

Weinberg, G. *Self Creation*. New York: Avon, 1978.

Zangwill, W. I. *Success with People: The Theory Z Approach to Mutual Achievement*. New York: Bantam, 1979.

Zenger, J., Miller, D., Florence, J. and Harlow, R. *How To Work For A Living And Like It: A Career Planning Workbook*. Reading, Massachusetts: Addison-Wesley, 1977.

Specifically for Career Changers

Bigg, D. *Breaking Out*. New York: David McKay, 1973.

Hiestand, D. L. *Changing Careers After Thirty-five*. New York: Columbia University Press, 1971.

Loughary, J. S. and Ripley, T. M. *Career And Life Planning Guide: How To Choose Your Job, How To Change Your Career, How To Manage Your Life*. Chicago: Follett, 1976.

Pearse, R. R. and Pelzer, B. P. *Self-Directed Change For The Mid-Career*. New York: AMACOM, 1975.

Stetson, D. *Starting Over*. New York: Macmillan, 1970.

For Women

Abarbanel, K. and Siegel, C. *Woman's Workbook*. New York: Praeger, 1975.

Ahern, D. D. with Bliss, B. *The Economics of Being a Woman*. New York: Macmillan, 1976.

Angrist, S. S. and Almquist, E. M. *Careers And Contingencies: How College Women Juggle With Gender*. Port Washington, New York: Kennikat Press, 1975.

Baldridge, L. *Juggling: The Art Of Balancing Marriage, Motherhood And A Career*. New York: Viking Press, 1976.

Bird, C. *Everything A Woman Needs To Know To Get Paid What She's Worth*. New York: Bantam Books, 1973.

Bird, C. *The Two Paycheck Marriage: How Women At Work Are Changing Life In America*. New York: Rawson, Wade, 1979.

Burack, E. H., Albrecht, M. and Seitler, H. *Growing: A Woman's Guide to Career Satisfaction*. Belmont, California: Lifetime Learning, 1980.

Clark, A. *New Ways to Work: A Gestalt Perspective*. San Francisco: Vitalia, 1975.

Curtis, J. *Working Mothers*. Garden City, New York: Doubleday, 1976.

Dunlap, J. *Personal And Professional Success For Women*. Englewood Cliffs, New Jersey: Prentice-Hall, 1972.

Epstein, C. F. *Woman's Place: Options And Limits In Professional Careers*. Berkeley, California: University of California Press, 1970.

Ginsberg, E. and Yohalem, A. M. *Corporate Lib: Women's Challenge To Management*, Baltimore, Maryland: The Johns Hopkins University Press, 1973.

Hall, F. S., and Hall, D. T. *The Two-Career Couple*. Reading, Massachusetts: Addison-Wesley, 1979.

Hennig, M. and Jardim, A. *The Managerial Woman*. New York: Doubleday, 1977.

Higginson, M. V. and Quick, T. L. *The Ambitious Woman's Guide To A Successful Career*. New York: AMACOM, 1975.

Jessup, C. and Chipps, G. *The Woman's Guide To Starting A Business*. New York: Holt Rinehart and Winston, 1976.

Jongeward, D. and Scott, D. *Affirmative Action For Women: A Practical Guide For Women & Management*. Reading, Massachusetts: Addision-Wesley, 1973.

Lembeck, R. *1001 Job Ideas For Today's Woman*. Garden City, New York: Dolphin Books Division of Doubleday, 1975.

Loring, R. and Wells, T. *Breakthrough: Women Into Management*. New York: Van Nostrand Reinhold, 1972.

Miller, G. P., Prince, J. S. and Scholz, N. T. *How To Decide: A Guide For Women*. Princeton, New Jersey: College Entrance Examination Board, 1975.

Nash, K. *Get The Best For Yourself: How To Discover Your Success Pattern And Make It Work For You*. New York: Grosset & Dunlap, 1976.

Pogrebin, L. C. *Getting Yours*. New York: David McKay Company, 1975.

Publications of the Women's Bureau. Washington, D.C.: U.S. Department of Labor, Workplace Standards Administration, Women's Bureau, 1971.

Schwartz, F., Schifter, M. and Gillotti, S. S. *How To Go To Work When Your Husband Is Against It, Your Children Aren't Old Enough And There's Nothing You Can Do Anyhow*. New York: Simon and Schuster, 1972.

Sommers, T. *The Not So Helpless Female*. New York: David McKay Company, 1973.

Splaver, S. *Non-Traditional Careers For Women*. New York: Messner, 1973.

Welch, M. S. *Networking: The Great New Way For Women To Get Ahead*. New York: Harcourt Brace Jovanovich, 1980.

Self-Employment

Biggs, D. *Breaking Out*. New York: David McKay Company, 1973.

Matthews, K. *On Your Own: 99 Alternatives To A 9 To 5 Job*. New York: Random House, 1977.

Weaver, P. *You, Inc.: A Detailed Escape Route To Being Your Own Boss*. New York: Doubleday, 1975.

Resumes

Angel, J. *Why And How To Prepare An Effective Job Resume*. New York: World Trade, 1972.

Bolles, R. N. *Tea Leaves: A New Look At Resumes*. Berkeley, California: Ten Speed Press, 1976.

Nutter, C. *The Resume Workbook: A Personal Career File For Job Applications*. Cranston, Rhode Island: The Carroll Press, 1970.

Poetry Index